BALTIC LITERATURE

BALTIC LITERATURE

A Survey of

Finnish, Estonian, Latvian, and Lithuanian Literatures

 ALEKSIS RUBULIS

THE UNIVERSITY OF NOTRE DAME PRESS
NOTRE DAME   LONDON

Library of Congress Catalog Card Number: 79–105728
Manufactured in the United States of America by
NAPCO Graphic Arts, Inc., Milwaukee, Wisconsin

Acknowledgments

Acknowledgment is gratefully expressed to the following publishers for permission to reproduce their copyrighted material: Harvard University Press for the selections from *The Kalevala*, translated by Francis P. Magoun, copyright © 1963 by the President and fellows of Harvard College (Cambridge, Mass.); Werner Söderström Osakeyhtiö for Uuno Kailas' "The Guilty Man" and Katri Vala's "Flowering Earth" from *Life and Letters* LII (Jan. 1947); G. P. Putnam's Sons for the excerpt from Mika Waltari's *The Egyptian*, copyright © 1949 by Mika Waltari; *Stand* for Pentti Saarikoski's "Greek Sequence" from *Stand*, No. 4, 1965; University of Florida Press for Juhan Liiv's "I Would Take a Garland of Flowers," Ernst Enno's "She Came," and Gustav Suits' "My Island" from *Modern Estonian Poetry*, edited by W. K. Matthews (Gainesville, Fla., 1953); Voyages Press for "The Moon Wedded the Sun," "Far Along the Meadow," and "O Mother, My Heart and Life" from *The Green Oak*, edited by Algirdas Landsbergis and Clark Mills (New York, 1962); Lithuanian Days for the excerpts from K. Donelaitis' *The Seasons* (Los Angeles, 1967) and A. Baranauskas' *The Forest of Anykščiai* (Los Angeles, 1956); *Lituanus* for the excerpt from Vincas Krėvė's *Sons of Heaven and Earth* from *Lituanus* XIII, no. 3 (Fall 1965); Manyland Books for Antanas Vaičiulaitis' "Noon at a Country Inn" from the book by the same title, copyright © by Antanas Vaičiulaitis, (Woodhaven, N.Y., 1965) and for Stepas Zobars-

Preface

The literary traditions of Lithuania, Latvia, Estonia, and Finland are, in fact, unrivalled in beauty, wisdom, age, and number. The treasures of these nations, their ancient folk songs, served as models for Longfellow, Goethe, and Walter Scott; their unique grandeur attracted Chopin, Schumann, Sibelius, and Schubert. Many foreign scholars have discovered in them an immense, genuine reservoir for research.

On the terrain of these nations, Western and Eastern cultures clash, creating an atmosphere for original and interesting modern belles-lettres, the comprehension of which facilitates the interpretation of other literatures from a different perspective. Unfortunately, the Baltic contribution remains relatively unknown abroad, for scholars and publishers show preference to the literatures of politically and economically great peoples.

All of the aforesaid nations are united with the West in mentality, ethnology, culture, politics, and religion; yes, particularly religion, for both Catholicism and Protestantism brought literacy, published the first books, and introduced Italian, German, and French schools of thought, thus reinforcing the affinity. It was also religion that divided even the kindred Slavs and shifted many of them into the Western sphere— for example, Poland, for which Fyodor Tyutchev (1803–1873), a leading Russian poet and diplomat, branded that country Judas.

The affiliation of Finland is somewhat obscure. At times it is associated with Sweden, Norway and Denmark. The Embassy of Finland in Washington, D.C., stated that Finland does not belong geographically to Scandinavia. Anthropologically, it is closely related to Estonia, for Finns, Estonians, and Hungarians form the agglutinative Finno-Ugrian subfamily of the Uralic grouping. Due to this convergence, Finns have folklore in common with Estonians, which is reflected in the *Kalevala* as well as in the *Kalevipoeg*. The title *Baltic Literature* was chosen merely to associate the book with some area.

This brief survey, of course, presumes neither to give explicit analyses nor solely to present *chefs-d'oeuvre*. Its objective is to present the literatures in their variety and national flavor. The size of each section depends upon the available translations and copyrights.

Aleksis Rubulis
University of Notre Dame

Contents

FINNISH LITERATURE

Folklore

National Awakening

Romanticism

Young Finland

Realism

The Torchbearers

Exploring Trends

ESTONIAN LITERATURE

Folklore

The Age of Enlightenment

Realism

Neoromanticism

LATVIAN LITERATURE

Folklore

Early Works

National Literature

LITHUANIAN LITERATURE

Folklore

Early Writings

Romanticism and Symbolism

Literature in the Twentieth Century

Finnish Literature

Folklore

In contrast to the Finnish written literature, the folklore of Finland is rather old. It reveals the true mentality of the Finnish people, their daily work, their way of life, and their struggle with their enemies and with the cruel northern nature. Oral literature flourished following the introduction of Christianity. Through Sweden the medieval court epic penetrated into Finland, became assimilated and achieved popularity during the fourteenth century. Among the Christian legends the most exquisite one speaks of the Son of God, who placed the sun on a lower branch of a fir tree where it illuminated only the chosen, i.e., rich people. Answering the prayers of the poor folk, Christ lifted the sun to the top of the tree so that all mankind might equally enjoy its light.

Elias Lönnrot (1802–1884), late professor of Finnish at Helsinki University, composed an important work for the preservation and promotion of folklore. Beginning in 1828, he made numerous expeditions on foot collecting folk poems, riddles, proverbs, and incantations. Between 1836 and 1845 Lönnrot also traveled to Norway, Estonia, Latvia, and Russia to do research in linguistics. In 1835 he compiled the national epic, the *Kalevala,* which appeared in a revised and enlarged edition in 1849.

Etymologists have not been able to provide an explicit derivation of the term *Kalevala.* Christfrid Ganander's *Mythologia Fennica* (1789) identifies Kaleva as a rough giant of the North. The Lithuanian word *kalvis* and the Latvian *kalējs* mean "a blacksmith," who in ancient times was considered a strong and clever man, a hero. Estonians and Finns use the *ala* for a territory or province. In any case, the most cognizant explanation is "the land of Kalev" or "the land of heroes."

In the prologue Lönnrot explains that the purpose of the work is to pass on old traditions to future generations:

It is my desire,
　　it is my wish
to set out to sing,
　　to begin to recite,
to let a song of our clan glide on,
　　to sing a family lay.
The words are melting in my mouth,
　　utterances dropping out,
coming to my tongue,
　　being scattered about on my teeth.

Beloved friend, my boon companion,
　　my fair boyhood comrade,
start now to sing with me,
　　begin to recite together
now that we have come together,
　　have come from two directions.
Seldom do we come together,
　　meet one another
on these wretched marches,
　　these poor northern parts.

Let us clasp hand in hand,
　　fingers in fingers,[1]
so that we may sing fine things,
　　give voice to the best things
for those dear ones to hear,
　　for those desiring to know them
among the rising younger generation,
　　among the people which is growing up,
those songs about,
　　those lays inspired by

---

[1] Whenever two Finns sing folk songs, they sit, hands clasped together, and sway forwards and backwards. According to the *Kalevala*, Song 40, their singing is accompanied by the *kantele*, manufactured by Väinämöinen. Actually, this is also the Estonian national musical instrument *kannel*, the Latvian *kokle*, and the Lithuanian *kanklès*. Song 44:227-228 speaks of five, six, and seven strings. A large *kantele*, however, can have up to thirty strings.

old Väinämöinen's[2] belt,
    the depths of Ilmarinen's[3] forge,

the point of the sword of a man with a far-roving mind,
    the range of Joukahainen's[4] crossbow,
the remote corners of North Farm's[5] fields,
    the heaths of the Kaleva District.
These my father formerly sang
    while carving an ax handle,
these my mother taught me
    while turning her spindle,
me a child rolling on the floor
    in front of her knee,
miserable milkbeard,
    little clabbermouth.
There was no lack of songs in the Sampo
    nor did Louhi lack magic charms.
        (Francis P. Magoun, Jr.)

The plot consists mainly of Väinämöinen's and Ilmarinen's adventures visiting the beautiful girl of the North Farm, the forging of the magic Sampo and the fight for it. Sampo is a three-sided mill, one side of which produces grain, the other salt, and the third money, and it symbolizes prosperity. The mythic epic has charms for almost every occasion: hunting, fishing, skiing, exorcism, and the sauna (45:197–232):

He got a sauna good and hot,
    the stones producing vapor
heated with pieces of clean wood,
    with wood drifted in by the sea.
He brought water under his cloak,
    carried the bath whisks warily;

---

[2] A sage, magician, and bard.
[3] The smith who forged the Sampo, the arch of the sky, and a wife of gold.
[4] A bold young Lapp.
[5] A country governed by the witch Louhi, possibly Lapland. Louhi had a beautiful daughter, who was wooed by Väinämöinen and Ilmarinen.

he got whisks scalding hot,
  softened the bushy ones.
Then he produced honeyed vapor,
  raised honeyed vapor
through the hot stones,
  the glowing flat stones.
He speaks with these words,
  made this utterance:
"Come now, God, into the vapor,
  father of the sky, into the warmth
so as to bring about health,
  to establish peace.
Wipe away the sacred sparks,
  extinguish the sacred infections;
have bad vapor struck to the ground,
  send away evil vapor
so that it will not burn your sons,
  harm your offspring.
Whatever water I keep throwing
  on those hot stones,
may it be changed to honey,
  ooze out like honey.
Let a river of honey flow,
  let a pond of honey surge
through the pile of stones,
  through the moss-caulked sauna.
We will not be destroyed without cause
  nor killed except by natural diseases,
not without the permission of the great Creator,
  only by a death sent by God."
                    (Francis P. Magoun, Jr.)

The cure, however, does not depend merely upon prayer or superstition. The people apply water to cleanse wounds; they believe that flapping with a birch besom in the heat kills germs and promotes the circulation of blood. Illness appears as a real being, living in the air or water and, at times, on the earth, adopting the form of a bird, a cat or some other small animal. It can be also a punishment of God, inflicted by a sorcerer or devil.

Toward the end of the epic, Väinämöinen, being a pagan hero, vanishes, yielding to the son (Christ) of Marjatta (the Virgin Mary). The *Kalevala* does not exhibit the Homeric grandeur of expression found in the *Iliad* and the *Odyssey,* for Finnish runes were created and sung by peasants. On the other hand, it surpasses the Greek epics in individualization and in sturdy characterization. Unlike the *Iliad,* the *Odyssey,* and the *Nibelungenlied,* the *Kalevala* consistently values and reveres wisdom as the highest virtue.

The *Kalevala* consists mainly of one form, the four-foot trochee, which is identical with Longellow's poem *The Song of Hiawatha,* for Longfellow adopted its meter and even copied some passages. Sparse in rhyme but rich in alliteration and caesuras, the *Kalevala* is original in its structure and beauty, differing from the antique and classic as well as from modern literature. Like most epics, the *Kalevala* lacks unity. It is an amalgam, composed primarily of genuine epic poems sung by the peasants, some heroic tales, myths, legends, proverbs, with Lönnrot's written verses serving as a joinder. To maintain the rhythm, he inserted nonsense words. In the preface of the *Kalevala's* 1849 edition, Lönnrot confessed:

> Assiduous attempts have been made both to arrange the poems and to connect them one with the other as carefully and as correctly as possible, and to assemble in one work all information contained in these poems relating to the life, customs and events of those times. Some arbitrariness is, however, evident from the compilation of the work, due to the fact that even the best singers did not know a great number of successive poems, and those that they recited were not always quite uniform. For this reason, it has often been necessary to treat the subject according to its own particular nature, and even sometimes to depart from the sequence adhered to in the Old Kalevala.[6]

[6] Quoted by A. O. Väisänen in "The Origin of *Kalevala,*" *The Norseman* VII (1949), 133.

Lönnrot conjectured that the material originated more than one thousand years ago in Karelia. The Karelians were Orthodox at that time, but the poems apparently reveal Catholic traditions and expressions of the western dialects. Some scholars, therefore, attempt to prove their origin in the west.

The *Kalevala* is not the only literary tradition which served Finnish national interests. The folklore archives of the Finnish Literary Society contain some 80,000 narrative and lyric poems, 50,000 folk songs of a late type, 150,000 tales and fables, about a million proverbs and sayings, and 50,000 riddles.

 National Awakening

Although Cornelius Tacitus briefly alluded to the primitive Finnish culture in his book *Germania* (98 A.D.), the oldest extensive document concerning Finland is the papal bull of 1171 or 1172, which reports the propagation of Greek Orthodoxy in the eastern regions. In 1155, the Swedish King Erik the Good, aided by the English-born Bishop Henry, seized Finland and drew it into the Western cultural sphere. Although every citizen enjoyed equal privileges and responsibilities, Swedish became the official language in all public offices and in schools. Only religious services were conducted in the mother tongue.

Mikael Agricola (c. 1510–1557), who was a student of Luther and later bishop of Turku, brought the Reformation from Germany. He wrote the first ABC (c. 1540) and translated the New Testament into Finnish in 1548. The Bible was published in Finnish in 1642.

Sweden maintained a pro-British policy. In 1808–1809 the Russian emperor, Alexander I, under pressure from Napoleon, occupied Finland in an effort to force the Swedish king, Gustav Adolph IV, to adandon his friendship with England, Napoleon's chief enemy.

The war of 1808–1809 brought the first national awakening. Finland was converted into an autonomous grand duchy with its own constitution but under the control of the Russian Empire. Soon the publicist Adolf Ivar Arwidsson (1791–1858) challenged his people: "Swedes we are no longer; Russians we never can be; therefore we must become Finns."[7]

Jaakko Juteini (1781–1855) played a dominant role among the first pioneers for an independent Finnish heritage. Juteini's works, although feeble, are voluminous. His productivity in poetry, prose, and drama advanced the awakening and enlightenment of the peasantry. Carl Axel Gottlund (1796–1875) made an effort to influence the educated classes by publishing in Finnish various articles in the fields of literature and science. Several Finnish newspapers were established, and Jakob Fredrik Lagervall translated and localized Shakespeare's *Macbeth* in 1834.

A great patriot and leading poet throughout Scandinavia, Johan Ludvig Runeberg (1804–1877), contributed far more impressively to a national sentiment. Lacking fluency in the Finnish tongue, he expressed himself in Swedish. Nevertheless, his clear patriotic motives and the vividness of his characters led both Finns and Swedes to adopt many of his poems as folk songs. Some of them, e.g., "March of the Men of Björneberg," resounded during battles of the revolution of 1917–1918 while Finnish patriots fought the Red Guard. Runeberg's poem in nine cantos, *The Elk Hunters* (1832), portrays the cruel lives of the Finnish peasants, their struggles, amusements, and hunts for the elk and the bear. The first excerpt, taken from the fourth canto, describes the attempt of the bragging Russian peddler Ontrus to equate his money with the *integer vitae* of the poor Finnish girl Hedda, whom he courts for his younger brother Tobias:

> Stroking his beard and moustache, where the froth of the
>   beer had been settling,
> Ontrus did set about wooing the girl for his much-beloved
>   brother.
> "Hedda!" he shouted at once, when the housekeeping
>   chamber he entered,

[7] J. Hampden Jackson, *Finland* (New York, 1940), p. 54.

"Splendid he is, oh splendid, the handsomest lad of Arch-
angel;
Done! thou must take for thy husband the flourishing
lovely Tobias!
Seest thou how fat, and how round, and how rosy, his cheeks
and his lips are,
And how his beautiful hair, like the glossiest sable in value,
Shading his cheek and his neck, is even and low on the
forehead?
But on his chin, dost thou witness a crop of the quick-
sprouting beardie?
Soon, like a fox-tail, fluffy and long, it will fall on his jacket.
Splendid he is, oh splendid, the handsomest lad of Arch-
angel;
Done! thou must take for thy husband the flourishing,
lovely Tobias!
And, as to dancing, my friend, if of heels or of toes it's a
question,
No one can match him in falling as flat on the floor as an
'eight-cake,'
Neither in springing up, cutting his capers again, like a
rocket.
All in his dancing is perfect, if legs or if arms he is swinging,
If he is singing, or kicking, or stamping, or whistling, or
smiling.
Splendid he is, oh splendid, the handsomest lad of Arch-
angel;
Done! thou must take for thy husband the flourishing lovely
Tobias!
What, if carousing at times, we are lying drunk on the
flooring?
Only anon do we drink, oh seldom, but seldom, not always;
Chilly is winter, my girl, and heavy the wanderer's knap-
sack;
Having been starved at the stranger's, from fear of bur-
glars and brigands,

Beer do we drink, when to friends and customers paying
    a visit.
Splendid he is, oh splendid, the handsomest lad of Arch-
    angel;
Done! thou must take for thy husband the flourishing,
    lovely Tobias!
Come to Archangel; good is the ware-abundant Archangel:
Silk shall there be thy dress, and silver-roubles, thy board-
    ing.
Finland is poor, there is nothing but fells and forests in
    Finland.
Come, oh come to Archangel and live on the banks of
    the Dvina!
Rich is the brown-beard-flocculent Ontrus, rich is his
    brother!
Splendid he is, oh splendid, the handsomest lad of Arch-
    angel;
Done! thou must take for thy husband the flourishing, lovely
    Tobias!"

Thus he was pleading, at once from out of his bosom
    producing,
Big with bank-notes, a bag, he swung it up to the rafters.
Whirling like butterflies round, the bank-notes, easy and
    airy,
Reddish and whitish and blue, and in more than five thou-
    sand roubles,
Floatingly fell on the floor, and between them, and on them,
    among them,
Sprang with bright-flashing eyes, in enchanted audacity,
    Ontrus.

Meantime the sober and sensible Hedda went out of the
    chamber,
Left him to woo and dance by himself, and went to her
    mistress,

Who was counting her washing, and tidily writing a wash-
bill.
Smiling, she listened to Hedda and what, in the housekeep-
ing chamber,
Ontrus had shouted and done, and the story muddled her
reckoning.

Now that the brown-beard-flocculent Ontrus did see he
was single,
Love he forgot all at once, and soon made an end of his
capers.
Picking his notes from the floor with hands that were trembling with worship,
Kissing them each with delight, as thousands of times he
had kissed them,
Back in his bag he did put them, and sweetly grinning
he did it,
Round, as before, in his bosom, and then he went back to
the kitchen.

There Tobias was dancing away the throes of his passion,
Scarcely able to turn any more, in giddiness reeling,
Mixing laughter with tears, and loud lamentation with
rapture,
While, on staggering feet, he attempted to sing to his capers,
Until, deserted by head and by legs, he fell on the flooring,
Leaving the sores of his heart to be healed by merciful
slumber.

Such his appearance was now, when the brown-beard-
flocculent Ontrus
Came from his wooing-pursuits, and hummingly entered
the kitchen.
Two things dwelt in the mind of the entering pedlar.
Approaching,
Quickly, the table, he glanced with concern at the jug,
which was empty.
This he sent out, by a beard-covered one, to be filled with
the kalja,

Then, looking round, he was trying to think where his
  down-toppled comrade
Might get a place, that he should not, when lying prone
  on the flooring,
Be in the way of their feet, and hinder his dance and the
  others.
Fitting he found, as a couch for his sleeping brother, the
  pallet,
Nearest the fire-place, nicely provided with pillows of
  rushes,
Where now, reposing her wearying body, the aged Rebecca
Peacefully laid herself down, by the side of the grey-speckled
  pussie.
There was Ontrus now dragging his sleeping, beer-bur-
  dened brother,
Cheerfully smiling, when seeing how thoroughly sound was
  his slumber;
Then he fell down on his knees, and shook by the shoulders
  the old one:
"Move up a little, just move up, thou aged Rebecca," he
  pleaded,
"Nearer the wall, and chase the soft-purring cat from thy
  bosom,
That, instead, thou may'st have a flourishing laddie beside
  thee!"

"Fie!" upstarting, she cried, the limping, decrepit Rebecca,
"Beelzebub bridle thy blasphemous mouth, thou long-
  bearded ogre!
Could I enjoy e'en a wink of sleep, with his ungodly capers?
Could I expect any rest, if I lay here from even till even?
Woe to the ill-fated day that I saw thee, unchristian heathen,
Loathed in the country, go roaming about!" So saying,
  the woman
Flung, with shivering hands, the cat in the face of the
  Russian.
Frightened, the cat caught hold of his flocculent beard, with
  a sputter,

Scratching his cheek, and his chin, and leaped on the oven
    in a twinkling,
Where, in the dark, with glistening eyes, she soon began
    purring;
But, to repose, she calmly lay down, the aged Rebecca.
Ontrus, however, remained still stroking his chin with his
    fingers,
Grumbled, and swore by himself, alternately smiling, and
    wondering,
Till, for the beer, that was brought in at once, he forgot all
    his drawbacks;
Dragging Tobias away from the dangerous bed, he allotted
Unto his brother a place on the bench where he sat by the
    beer-jug.
Meanwhile, a shrill and unquenchable laughter, began by
    the maidens,
Rang by the silent spinning-wheels still, and the aged
    Rebecca
Started in bed, and calling her pussie, lay down for her
    night-rest.

                       (Anna Krook)

    The following realistic extract, from canto six, reveals the
hardship and misery which people had to endure. At times their
struggle for survival ended in tragedy:

"Now, if thou wishest to hear, thou much-knowing Anna,
    my story,
Well, I will tell thee at once, in truth, how all of it
    happened.
Kangas, my farm, is in Soini, a farm like four to be valued,
Wooded, wealthy in corn-fields, and lakes and grass-covered
    beaches.
Unto my father it came when he married its flourishing
    daughter;
There did he live and grow grey, like a summer's even to
    look at.
Then it was left by my father to me. My hair was beginning

Also to blanch, where I sat like a king, at the fruit-bearing
  Kangas.
Servants I boasted of, stalwart men at the plough and the
  hatchet,
Maids in the kitchen, besides; and sons and daughters,
  their mother's
Comfort, the hope of my old age, growing like saplings
  around me.
So did I sit there, easily paying my taxes and burdens
Year after year, and envied by many, by all men com-
  mended,
Until misfortune did come and destroyed my gladness. A
  frost-night
Spoilt all my corn, unharvested yet; wild beasts were
  attacking,
Bleeding my flocks. Thus passed the following winter in
  trouble.
Borrowing rye for sowing, I meant to repay it in autumn;
Autumn gave me no rye, but the corn-ears, an icicle-coating.
Servants and maidens deserted my farm, unpaid were the
  taxes,
Life was craving for bread—in the oven, bark only was
  drying.
Days and weeks, though, wore on; as long as the kine, that
  were left us,
Still were giving us milk, did the bark go down and sus-
  tain us.
Thus passed the Yule-tide away; though pining, we held
  out, however.
But one day when I came from the woods, with a bark-
  burden loaded,
Greeted I was by some men at my door, 'Friend,' one of
  them uttered,
'Pay thy debt, lest thou lose here today, by extent, thy
  belongings!'
Taken aback, I replied: 'Give it up, oh much-honoured
  master;

Let me pay off when the Lord will render me able! On
    bark-bread
Now we are living.' Replying no word, they went back to
    the kitchen,
Took from the walls my meagre deposit of tools and
    utensils,
And what was left us of clothes, then carried them out to
    the sledges.
Weeping, she sat in the bedstead on straw, my much-valued
    good-wife,
Looking at us, but in silence, and trying now only to
    comfort
Baby that wailingly lay on her bosom, a day old and
    helpless.
Leaving the house with the men with the last things worthy
    of pawning,
Stiff did I feel like the pine when the axes boom at its
    root-stem.
But when I came to the yard, they valued their booty;
    it did not
Cover e'en half of my debt. 'My friend,' now repeated the
    Bailiff,
'Little is this, but hast thou not milk-yielding kine in thy
    byre?'
Saying these words, they proceeded to find out the kine,
    Which was easy,
As they were standing in stalls and bellowing, lacking their
    fodder.
Soon the kine were unbound, and let out, one after the
    other,
Making resistance, unruly, and leaving their byre with
    sorrow.
Six were led to the sledges, the seventh, which, meagre and
    feeble,
Restive, refused to go with them, was left me: then all of
    them started.
Silently wandering back to the house, I entered the kitchen.

'Aaron, my friend,' these words now uttered my wife in her
   bedstead,
'See that a something I get to quench my hunger, a milk-
   drop
Were to me so sweet; I'm thirsty and have no food for my
   baby.'
Thus she was murmuring. Darkness fell on mine eye and
   with trouble
Only I got to the byre. There, hanging her head, did the
   creature
Stand and chew at some straw in her sorrow; the hard-
   drying udder's
Dugs with my shivering hands I seized, alternately trying
Now at the one, now the other—but all was in vain, not
   a milk-drop
Did they bestow. Despairing, I pressed at them harder, but
   blood-drops
Forced themselves out, with red, besprinkling the depth of
   the milk-pail.
Furious now, like the bear, when pierced by the spear is
   his bosom,
Into the kitchen I ran, and tearing a cake from the bread-
   spit,
Cut it a blow with my axe, and black flew the bark from
   its fissures.
Then to my wife the pieces I carried: 'See here, what is
   left us.'
'Eat this,' I muttered, 'and satiate thy child!' One piece
   she accepted,
Turned it in silence round in her hand, looked on it,
   and clasping
Unto her bosom the babe, she fell in a swoon on the
   corn-sheaf.
Snow-skates I put on my feet in a haste, and flew to my
   neighbour's,
He who nearest me dwelt, a pipe's way, if in a hurry;

When at his house I arrived and asked for a soothing assist-
   ance,
Brotherly sharing with me, he gave what he then had been
   saving.
Back did I bundle on home with some milk in a flask on
   my shoulders,
Gaining the farm-yard, gaining the kitchen. A sorrowful
   wailing
Met me at once; I entered and saw of my children, the eldest
Two, who weeping aloud, were surrounding their mother,
   and one babe
Shaking her soft by the hand, and the other, her head with
   its ringlets;
But immovable, dumb, she lay, death's snow-wreath was
   spreading
Over her stiffened cheek, and night on her eye-lids de-
   scending.
So it was all at an end, and wasted, my beautiful Kangas.
Then towards heaven I lifted my hands, and afterwards
   taking
Hold of my staff, I set off; on a sled, the children behind me
Dragging, now gray-haired, I went from parish to parish
   a-begging.
Time heals sorrow, however, and now, in the houses of
   strangers,
Flourish my much-beloved children anew; but myself with
   contented
Mind, am begging my bread and playing my harp, as the
   cricket
Sits, though the sunlight is scant, and sings on the withering
   leaflet.''

(Anna Krook)

Working as a teacher of the classics, Runeberg wrote, in his
leisure time, the famous cycle of poems *The Songs of Ensign
Stal* (1848), a refined chronicle of the military forces that
fought the Russians in 1808–1809. The opening poem of the

series, "Our Land," was set to music by Fredrik Pacius and became the Finnish national anthem. Runeberg's epic, *King Fjalar* (1844), deals with the discord between Viking desires and the commandments of God.

Even now Finns have not forgotten the unceasing struggle of the philosopher and senator Johan Vilhelm Snellman (1806–1881) to preserve their mother tongue. As the greatest statesman of the period of autonomy, Snellman was highly respected in St. Petersburg. Using his authority, he strongly opposed the Russification of Finland and demanded the recognition of the Finnish language in public offices and in schools, as well as the constitutional rights of the citizens. For his efforts he was threatened with banishment to Siberia. His endeavors led to the founding of the first Finnish secondary school in 1858. Snellman appealed to his nation:

> When the educated people of a country . . . speak one language and the rest of the nation, the masses, speak another, the language of the educated class has no power of survival. . . . What is required is that the educated people of our country are truly capable of being what they ostensibly are, the educated class of the Finnish nation of Finland.[8]

From 1856 till 1863 Snellman was a professor at Helsinki University.

The Tsar Nicholas II proclaimed that he was entitled to enact laws enforceable in Finland on any matter involving the interests of Russia, disregarding the Finnish Diet.[9] The imposition of Russian as the only official language began in 1899. The Constitutionalists considered the tsar's order illegal and called upon the nation to block the enactment, using violence if necessary. The governor-general, Babrikov, was assassinated, and the Constitutionalists and workers threatened to organize a strike on the national level. Aware of his temporary weakness, Nicholas II endorsed a more moderate policy.

Every one of these patriots helped to create an atmosphere

---

[8] Eino Jutikkala, *A History of Finland* (New York, 1962), p. 203.
[9] See Urho Toivola's *Introduction to Finland* (Helsinki, 1960), pp. 24–32.

vital for the rising of the nation. Lönnrot's *Kalevala,* however, was the strongest foundation-stone of Finnish literature. In this respect it was of even greater significance than Homer's *Iliad* and *Odyssey.* Finns of the educated class had adopted the Swedish language and had thus become estranged from their people. This national epic expressed Finnish ethnological characteristics, aroused national pride, and consolidated the nation.

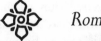 *Romanticism*

The romantic movement in Finnish literature began to prosper toward the end of the nineteenth century. The aforesaid literary and political figures prepared a fertile soil for the birth of modern Finnish literature, sounding in the musical mother tongue. The language transition, however, was carried out by Aleksis Kivi (1834–1872), whose style expressed realistic characteristics as well as adherence to the romantic movement.

Aleksis Kivi (whose real name was A. Stenvall) was born into a poor tailor's family in the parish of Nurmijärvi. He struggled through the lyceum and, in 1857, enrolled in the Helsinki University to study philosophy, a pursuit which was interrupted because of poverty and sickness. Using the Bible and the *Kalevala* for his keystones, and the works of Homer, Shakespeare, Cervantes, and Holberg for his lessons in the cottage of his patroness, Miss Charlotte Lönnkvist, Kivi contributed works which hold a prominent place in world literature. His masterpiece, *Seven Brothers* (1870), was the first novel written in the Finnish language. The intriguing plot depicts typical episodes in the rugged rural life of that time. After the death of their parents, the seven ignorant Jukola brothers reject education and, escaping from civilization, search for freedom in a wilderness, where they build themselves a cabin:

> The proper time arrived for hunting bears. The brothers seized their daggers, loaded their rifles with powerful cartridges and set out to awaken the chief of the woods, who

already lay dreaming in his dark den, deep under snow-covered spruce. Their weapons had felled many a strong-jowled bear when he, roaring furiously, crawled out from his hiding place. A cruel battle began; the snow whirled around and reddened with blood, for both sides suffered injury. Thus they fought until the vicious beast lay on the ground. Having luckily reached home with their booty, the brothers applied to their wounds an ointment which they made of alcohol, gunpowder, and brimstone. They then sealed the whole with yellow tar.

Thus the brothers secured provision from the forest as well as from the shrubbery on the hills, filling their storage with various game: wildfowl, hares, badgers, and the meat of bears. Finally, they laid in a supply of winter fodder for their old and faithful Valko.[10] On the verge of the marsh towered a huge haystack, harvested earlier with sickles and sufficient for the whole winter season. Nor was the fuel supply neglected. Beside the granary a mighty stack of firewood rose aloft above the ground, and closer to the cabin a heap of resinous stumps reached the roof. Thus prepared, they could expect the most severe winter, untroubled.

(Aleksis Rubulis)

Kivi believes in the resurrection of his characters, in the victory of culture over the raw nature of a man. All of the brothers return to modern society, becoming decent and respected farmers and the heads of families, as is witnessed by the parish hymnleader:

"Whether it was the devil who lured them into the wilderness, as once he enticed the parson of Tuusula away, or whether they were led by the heavenly power, like John the Baptist, I shall not clarify today. However, the devil did his utmost to drive them to destruction. He tempted them with poisonous alcohol; yes, he drove them even with sweet syrup; he ensnared them, as they themselves have explained, toward giddy heights, into a strange edifice called The Tower of Boot-leather, where he showed them half of the world in the

[10] The name of their horse.

most horrifying chaos in order to drive sanity from their human brains. He desired to achieve this end, but his own evil strategy disgraced him, for all the brothers found a true path at the right time. They engaged in a vigorous battle, struggling against their own hearts, against deep-rooted laziness, rocky fields, cold swamps and shoals, until their unyielding will and the help of our Lord of Sabaoth brought them triumph. Yea! And now they have returned to civilization again, not as robbers, but as honest and upright men. Now, solemnly and respectfully, they arrive at our village in their cart drawn by two lofty mares and followed by several stout cows and a bellowing, chubby-faced bull. Thus, they come, not as criminals from a cave where they would hide, but from the beautiful Impivaara's farmstead, which they made with their own hands. Yes, indeed! Through them the Lord of Sabaoth has been glorified and the horned Satan in hell put to shame."

(Aleksis Rubulis)

The style of the novel is interspersed with biblical decline followed by a sudden rise for the attainment of the most forcefull effect and incorporates Homeric comparisons and epithets. Aleksis Kivi spent nine years writing this epic of Finnish country life. Contemporary critics attacked the *Seven Brothers* severely, grieving the sick author and hastening his death. Nevertheless, the highly original novel became a best seller.

This man of varied talent is also a founder of the Finnish theater. In 1864, Kivi finished *Kullervo,* the first Finnish tragedy. It is based upon the *Kalevala* and made its author famous. His comedy *The Cobblers,* an excellent and witty character portrayal, appeared in the same year. This farce became a favorite stage play, won the government's award, and was filmed in 1938. The humorous one-act play *The Engagement* (1866) is still popular as a curtain raiser. The lyrical drama *Lea* (1869) has a biblical background and reveals the playwright's religious inspiration. Kivi was also a noted short story writer and a poet of considerable distinction. Indigence and solitude, however, plunged this striving man of letters into melancholy. Alcohol failed to provide the desired remedy, and in 1871 his career was ended when he suffered a mental breakdown.

During the intensified Russian oppression, Juhani Aho (Johan Brofeldt, 1861–1921) emerged and raised his voice to encourage resistance among Finnish patriots. However, he soon withdrew from politics. Although he became acquainted with French Naturalism and Impressionism while in Paris in 1889, Aho began his career as a devotee of realism, then switched to neoromanticism. He made his debut with the miniature novel *The Railroad* (1884), depicting the mechanization of a remote countryside. His historical novel *Panu* (1897) expresses ethnic characteristics. In the psychological novel *Juha* (1911), the writer describes the grief of a dedicated farmer, Juha, whose young wife, Marja, has run off with a smooth-tongued man. Aho liked to treat conflicts between the Christian and heathen traditions, a practice apparently borrowed later by Selma Lagerlöf. His portrayals of the Finnish lake country contain striking effects.

Beginning in 1872, the classical reportoires, the dramas of Shakespeare, Molière, Ibsen and Kivi, were performed at the Finnish National Theater under the supervision of its director, Kaarlo Bergbom (d. 1906). A great boost to the national stage were Minna Canth's dramas, *The Robbery Holdup* (1882), *A Workman's Wife* (1884), *A Priest's Family* (1892), *Sylvi* (1893), and *Anna Liisa* (1895). In her dramas this outstanding woman playwright promoted social justice for the poor, particularly women. Her narrative *A Selection of Novels* (1894) displays this same tendency.

 ## Young Finland

Toward the end of the nineteenth century, the literary school Young Finland originated. This organization strove to create a national artistic culture. Among the chief participants was Jean Sibelius (1865–1957), who composed many works inspired by mythology and national romanticism, e.g., *Finlandia,* the famous symphonic poem whose intrinsic musical merit serves as a symbol of Finnish nationalism; *A Saga,* a tone poem for orchestra; *Voces Intimae,* composition for string quartet; the cantata *Kullervo,* and *The Carelia Suite.* The painter Akseli Gallen-Kallela (1865–1931), influenced by the *Kalevala* as well as by the poets Leino, Aho, Manninen, and Koskenniemi, changed his style from naturalism to romantic realism.

The most gifted literary figure of the Young Finland movement and the greatest prodigy among Finnish poets of all time was Eino Leino (pen name of Armas Eino Leopold Lönnbohm, 1878–1926), who produced some thirty volumes of poetry and a number of plays, novels, and short stories. At the age of eighteen he published the collection *March Songs* (1896). Although this first volume disclosed the influence of Runeberg and Topelius, it clearly manifested the poet's eloquence, sturdy form, and vigorous intellect. After his study at Helsinki University and a wide reading of Goethe's and Schiller's ballads, Leino contrived his own individual lyric and narrative style. His capital work is the two-volume cycle of mythic poems *Songs at the Whitsun Fires* (1903), written in the strict meter of Finnish folklore. The 1905 revolution attracted Leino to politics. He dedicated his novel *Jaana Rönty* (1907) to the reactionaries. The volumes of his poetry *The Winter Night* (1905) and *Frosts* (1908) treat philosophical as well as social problems. Leino's milieu drama, *The Salt of the Earth* (1911), analyzes contemporary Finnish intelligentsia. He made a considerable contribution to the theater by writing a series of a half-dozen plays, *Masks* (1905–1911), and the cycle *Kalevala on the Stage* (1911). Eino Leino's narrative *The Honey Claw* (1914) resembles Heine's *Atta Troll* (1841) in that both of them call for a rebellion. His ballad *Ylermi* reveals imitation of Nietzsche's superman, for the knight Ylermi is endowed with the whims of Zarathustra.

Väinämöinen's Song (1905)

Not many the joys the gods have granted to mortals:
The joy of spring-time,

The summer's sweetness,
And lastly the time of the autumn, the high and
    transparent.
To plough and to sow, then
Heap up the harvest,
Find at last peace and rest one's reward after labour.

Not many are the sorrows the gods have granted to
    mortals:
Heart-sore the first sorrow,
Subsistence the second,
And death, the august and exalted, ever the third sorrow.
Friends will prove false to us,
Life, too, will leave us,
Magic's the hero's only might and achievement.

Why should I sing then, I to whom song has been given,
Any other joys or
Any other sorrows?
Unskilled am I in telling the tale of star-systems,
Or fishes of the sea-deeps,
Or flowers that the fields grow.
Sing will I then what man has been given to sing of.
Knowledge and skill are not for the hero to sing
Or present to the people.
Subjects to sing of

Are for the singer the changing years and the seasons,
The kindling of life-sparks,
And the extinguishing,
And the procession obeying life's and death's laws.

Everything else is but bright rainbow gleams under
    heaven's vault,
Glistening cat's-gold,
Wave-ripple reflection.
The hero shall sing his song as the sea sings,
Powerful, holy,
Awe-inspiring,
Gentle as restful night o'er earth's lands reposing.

Songs there are many and many are the minstrels.
One is the song that shall
Win all others:
The august song that sings of man, the ideal, the spirit.
Away pass peoples,
Not pass shall the power
Sung by the man that has mastered the soul of his people.

(Cid Erik Tallqvist)

Symbolism and perfection in form were represented at this time by the lyricist Otto Manninen (1872–1950), a professor at Helsinki University. He achieved wide recognition translating into Finnish the works of Homer, Sophocles, Euripidis, Goethe, Molière, Heine, Petöfi, Runeberg, and Ibsen. A stern self-criticism limited his output, while his released works evince formal refinement, ethical depth, and harmony.

The first Finnish philosophical poet was Veikko Antero Koskenniemi (V. A. Forsnäs, 1885–1962). Finland, night, fate, and death were his most cherished themes, pessimistically displayed in the volumes *Collected Poems* (1930) and *New Poems* (1943). As a professor of literature and a critic, Koskenniemi introduced classicism into Finnish literature.

Another significant literary figure of this movement was Zachris Topelius (1818–1898), a professor of history at Helsinki University and a rector from 1875 to 1878. Topelius' chief contribution is the ·historical novel *Tales of the Barber-Surgeon* (1853), an excellent portrayal of Finland during the seventeenth and eighteenth centuries. Basically, he was a writer of juvenile literature. Legendary motifs also occur in his romantic poetry:

The Milky Way

My waning lamp has been put out, but the night is
    calm and clear;
Now all the memories of old arise from far and near,
And gentle legends float about, like cloudlets in the
    wind.
I'm quivering with wistfulness and sorrowful in mind.

The twinkling stars are looking down, in winter's
    frosty gleam;
As though there were no death on earth, so blissfully
    they beam.
Know'st thou their silent voices all? Oh listen now
    to me,
I learnt a legend from the stars, and I will tell it thee.

He, in the glorious evening sky, in a distant star abode;
She lived in quite another star, and on another road.
And Zulamith, this was his name, and hers was Salome,
And all the fondest love they felt, would for each
    other be.

On earth they both had lived before and loved long,
    long ago,
But parted were by night and death, and grief, and sin
    and woe.
At last Death gave them shining wings, and peace and
    rest, but far,
One from the other now was doomed to live in a dif-
    ferent star.

But in their homes of eternal blue, they of each other
    thought.
Immense was the Creator's world of suns between them
    brought.
An endless world of stars, the wonders of His Mighty
    Hand,
In hopeless distance stretched between, an infinite,
    boundless land.

But Zulamith, consumed with love and longing, once
    begun
To build a bridge of sparkling light, of stars, from sun
    to sun;
And Salome commenced to build, like Zulamith, from
    afar,

A bridge of starlight from her strand, a bridge from
 star to star.

For a thousand years they built and built, with never-
 failing faith,
"And thus the Milky Way was built," is what the
 legend saith,
The bridge that clasps the highest arch of heaven, the
 Zodiac's race,
And binds together strand with strand across the sea
 of space.

Dismay seized all the Cherubs now; to God there flew
 a horde—
"What Salome and Zulamith have built, now see, O
 Lord!"
But God Almighty smiled, and rays were streaming
 from His Crown—
"What faithful love built in My world, I never shall
 pull down."

And Salome and Zulamith, now that the bridge was
 done,
Sprang right into each other's arms, and then a star,
 or sun,
Rose in the highest arch of heaven—none was so clear
 and sweet—
Thus, after years of deadening pain, our hearts with
 joy may beat.

And all who love on this dark earth with a love so fond
 and bright,
But parted are by sin and grief, and woe, and death,
 and night,
Can they but build a bridge of love, from world to
 world, a way,
Be sure their love shall reach its aim, their longing,
 peace for aye.

         (Anna Krook)

Realism

German, English, French, Swedish, and Russian literature penetrated the Finnish mind. Rigid national consciousness was gradually softened by emphasis on individual freedom. New works came into existence in which a single human being revolted against the prevailing social norms. The impulsive novelist Volter Adalbert Kilpi (pseudonym of Volter Erikson, 1874–1939) heralded his original but subjective concepts in the volumes of his prose poems *Bathsheba* (1900), *Parsifal* (1902), and *Antinoüs* (1903). At this point he abandoned neoromanticism and decadence. In a narrative trilogy, *In the Hall of the Estate Alastalo* (1933), he depicts his native countryside with techniques similar to those of James Joyce and Marcel Proust. The same methods were employed in his anthology of stories, *Little People of the Parish* (1934).

True individualists bearing typical Finnish images were critically presented by Maila Talvio (assumed name of M. Mikkola, 1871–1952) in her trilogy, *The Daughter of the Baltic Sea* (1929–1936), an analytical fresco of Helsinki. Johannes Linnankoski (pseudonym of Juho Vihtori Peltonen, 1869–1913) accepted poetic realism while young. Only his biblical drama *The Eternal Struggle* (1903) displays a romantic tendency in the combat between good and evil. Strong realistic traits are discernible in his novel in verse *The Song of the Fire-Red Flower* (1905), which relates the adventures of a local dissolute raftsman. Realism was reinforced in Linnankoski's *Fugitives* (1908) and other psychological novels which hail nature, the integrity of man, and youth.

The foremost prose writer of the realistic movement was Frans Eemil Sillanpää (1888–1964), a winner of the Nobel Prize in 1939. His first novel, *The Sun of Life* (1916), follows in the tradition of the *Kalevala* and of Aleksis Kivi in glorifying the sun, an entity especially dear to every northerner. His artistry of language and his portrayal of the love affair of two youngsters attracted a wide audience for the book. Sillanpää's discursive sentences can be attributed to his fondness for Knut Hamsun. In the intense novel *Meek Heritage* (1919), outlined against a revolutionary background, the tragic protagonist Jussi and the loose-natured maid Rina beget an illegitimate child and experience many kinds of difficulties. Jussi is accused of deserting his sentry duty and is executed. While the work maintains clear vision and serenity, it is penetrated with melancholy. Sillanpää's naturalistic philosophy affirms indifference toward birth and death. An innate affinity between two people is portrayed in his *The Way of Man* (1932). Sillanpää secured international fame with the publication of *Fallen Asleep While Young* (1932), which reveals the anguish of the forsaken servant girl, Silja:

> The spring came when Silja would have to pass her Confirmation class. From Kustaa's dwelling to the church the distance was about six miles, so that he had to find lodgings where she could sleep on weekday nights. There were many girls in the same situation; they lodged in groups in the village houses and assembled in the evenings on the bridge and the quay, conscious of the clumsy remarks and coarse bursts of laughter from boys of like age and a little older. Some of the girls already felt a strong inclination for such company. They gave back as good as they received. And even the minds of the shyest were moved by certain hitherto dimly perceived matters. They were on the threshold of maidenhood. The summer that now unfolded from day to evening in the open spaces around the church was to be their first summer of liberty, during the course of which many were already to experience why they had been born women.
>
> When Saturday evening came they could be seen happily trudging away along all the roads leading from the village. At cross-roads they stopped and chattered a while before parting, in that, too, resembling older women in a faintly ludicrous manner. For the boys of Confirmation age, partings at crossroads were of a very different character: bold impertinences were shouted at boys from other hamlets; stones flew, and sometimes, on suitable occasions, a group would be

chased, when blood flowed freely from noses that had tended
to tilt too far skyward in the churchyard and on the village
paths in the evenings. There no one had dared to fight for
fear of the constable and the curates.

The girls walked as became young women; a few of the
farmers from the most distant hamlets had left their trip
to the village to Saturday afternoon, and now the daughter
would be perched up on the trap beside her stout father on
her way home for Sunday. Cries were exchanged between the
girls too, between those on foot and those driving, but these
cries were merry and decently worded. The evening rays
seemed to rejoice in the flashing of eyes and the gleam of teeth.

On one road Silja Salmleus walked homeward, first with
two companions, then with one, and after the departure of
this last friend, alone. Her father could see her coming
nearer. He stood beside the wood-pile and chopped fuel for
the bathhouse. Silja came, cast an open glance at her father,
but said no word of greeting as she passed him on her way
inside. The strokes of Kustaa's axe echoed and the billets
crackled; it was a delightful Saturday evening in early summer. Then Silja came out of the house in familiar working
dress. She came straight to her father and asked him for
something to do, though she knew quite well what there was
to be done.

"Take the wood in and make a fire, and we'll get it over
all the earlier," said Kustaa.

Their voices had exchanged greetings. The Saturday evening work passed smoothly for the couple, father and daughter, joined together by a warm mutual feeling. A feeling of
deep human happiness, from which, as the years passed, everything inessential or disturbing had fallen away.

Not until they had returned from the bath-house, and
Kustaa sat in his shirt-sleeves beside the back window, comb-
ing his still thick hair before a mirror, and Silja flitted about
the range like a pale ghost of evening, did they begin to dis-
cuss anything. The father asked over his shoulder how she
liked her lodgings, the family being unknown to him. If anything she said was not quite to his liking, he did not stop to
explain it to the girl, but went on asking and commenting in
such a way that the conversation between father and daugh-

ter revealed that both were of one mind. There he sat, her
father; the girl caught a glimpse now and again of his strong
and fine profile against the window as she had once done in
her childhood, while in bed with fever. Then the man got
into the bed and said no more to his daughter, and did not
even seem to be following her movements. Silence had settled
down on the room; one could almost feel the dignified evening thoughts of the man in the air.

Softly, as though gliding, and taking care not to rattle the
door, the daughter went out into the yard, still wrapped in
the spring-like twilight of early summer. The flowering bird-
cherry bushes on the distant bank and along the roads beyond
the lake seemed to be floating in that dimness. The birds
gradually grew silent near the house, but in the crowns of the
farther backwoods one could guess that some of the bigger
songsters were giving voice in long, long melodies to the
deepest meaning of the northern summer night, for which
they had so cheerily come so far. There were nests already,
and in them eggs—the depicter of the northern summer
night soon finds himself under the spell of well-worn phrases.
Under the pallid sky in the dimness flowers, the fading music of Nature, somewhere a solitary maiden—Silja Salmelus
stood and moved, listening to and sensing the summer night.

She moved gradually to the end of the point of land on their
own part of the shore, to the leafy verge of the bank, and sat
down there on the trunk of a birch, bent near the roots. Her
young mind seemed to expand and grow bolder. No one and
nothing could disturb her there. Yonder in the house, within
hearing, her father slept lightly, and no path led past here.

The water with its shores and islands rested as in a picture she had once seen. In the water the reflections repeated
towards the depths all that rose to the heights on the banks.
Everything the senses could grasp seemed to be gravely and
eagerly assuring the consciousness of its goodness, to be whispering to the girl, that "If you still sigh for anything all we
can do is to soothe your longing with what you now see."
This direct message from Nature made the girl's eyes expand,
as though they too, like the lake, had wanted to reflect in
their depths everything in view. There was much the sixteen-
year-old girl might have sighed for, something she might

have owned, and knew from hearsay had been hers, though she had never consciously missed it. That was perhaps why her eyes, having expanded, grew slightly moist and her breast heaved in a gentle sigh on this night on which she had come home from her Confirmation class to see her lonely father. Yes, he was lonely, the old man sleeping in the cabin. The thought lent support to her own melancholy; she felt herself his safeguard. Silja looked into her own being and saw that she was a woman.

The night grew deeper. Silja rose and took a few steps towards the shore, intending to climb back a little later to the house. She would have liked to stay too: in some way the landscape became imbued with a stronger life as a boat came forward from behind an island, travelling apparently from south to north. The rhythm of the oars revealed the rower's mood: how the summer night had taken possession of it, deciding the direction in which thought should run and thereby the interval between the strokes. The approaching sound did not disturb, only interpreted. Silja gathered a flower from the ground, without intending to do so, and looked sidelong at the oncoming boat. The rower let his oars rest, as though in answer to the girl's movement, although it was almost impossible that he could have seen her. He seemed after all to be no real traveller but only a lonely spectator of the night, a youth, apparently unknown, in clothes that were neither working-clothes nor holiday attire, that she could distinguish, a summer visitor from one of the distant villas, boating. Silja was quite certain she had seen him, some weekday in the village, on a bicycle. That was why she could make out his clothes at this distance. His nose was slightly hooked and his front teeth showed easily when he spoke to the baker's wife. Yes, it was he, right opposite her now, so that they might be looking each other in the eye. Silja made a few plucking motions at her flower, the brown eyes looked forth once or twice under the long lashes, then the girl began moving towards the house in such fashion that each step was like a separate little event, a confirmation of something. As she went the girl did not fail to note that the youth still rested on his oars, there behind her back. Not until the girl had been in the shadow of the foliage for some time, wholly invisible from the lake, did she hear the youth make a few strokes and then wait again for a moment or two, and when at last he started to row away the rhythm of his oars was unlike what it was when he came.

The night would by now be at its deepest. How long had she lingered near the water? As Silja came into the cabin she herself was aware that she brought with her in the folds of her dress a faint breath of the perfume of the night air. The flower was still in her hand. She felt like saving everything that had accompanied her from outside.

Sleep seemed unwilling to come even now, so she sat down at the side window, from which she had a view over the fields towards the village. So wonderful the night was, the first of its kind for Silja in her life so far. In the rear corner of the bed she could distinguish the white-clad figure of a man: father usually slept uncovered. Silja gazed in his direction and somehow the way in which she now looked at him surprised her. Father was an old man, who had been through much in his life, so she had been told. My lot is cast here with that old man, he is my father. What does it mean?

Her father slept on his back, motionless. Even his breathing was inaudible: there was something mildly terrifying in him. Silja remembered that her grandfather had been found dead in the threshing-barn; no one had seen the manner of his end. Was father awake, although he said nothing? Silja could not ask him, nor could she go nearer to make sure. She looked in turn out of all of the three windows. Everywhere the night met her, seeming now much emptier than a while ago. On the lake the reflections had grown dim.

At last came a movement from the bed and a faint sound as of choked coughing. Her father rose to a sitting position and then went over to the window giving on the point. Leaning against the window-frame he remained there moveless for a few moments. Then, sighing, he turned, and saw Silja at the other side of the room.

"Ah—have you come in," the old man said in a sleep-befuddled voice and went to bed again. Silja grasped that he had not seen her when he got up from the bed.

In the corner of the room the slender figure of the girl could be seen noiselessly moving, turning gradually white and disappearing into the bed. Sleep had fallen over the house. Outside here was no further sound of oars for long. Only a brief moment was left to the dawn of the approaching Sunday morning.

And yet, how beautiful an ordinary country church is on a Sunday morning in midsummer, when the heavens are calm and cloudless and all the growth of the earth is attaining the height of its luxuriance, at the moment before Man sharpens his scythe to mow it down. On such Sundays people flock to the church who do not take much interest in religion during the week. In snowy-white shirt-sleeves the master bustles near the stable-door, shouting to the stable-boy who leads out the horse, before going to the shed to draw out the trap, the newness, neatness and polish of which he pauses to admire. He throws the harness over the back of his mare, now in her prime; soon the breast-strap has been tied, the tail-strap and girth adjusted, the reins secured to the bit—every action carried out swiftly and instinctively, so that the master is able while harnessing the horse to shout directions, if need be, to his men. He drops the reins and rushes to hasten on his wife, who emerges finally in her silk dress and hat, prayer-book and umbrella in hand, shouting, she too, a command to the cow-girl standing listlessly near the byre, and coming to the trap climbs into it, a little clumsily and as though critical of the whole outfit, the master's sole concern as they are. The master steps lightly into his seat on the right, and so the couple set off at a steady jog, between fields, their own and those of other farms, soon those of another hamlet, up and down the low hills. As they draw near a cross-roads, they see through the shimmering morning heat and over the level green of a rye-field the approach of a similar couple from another farm. The horse and those in the trap are easily recognised, but there is no call to start shouting to each other, even though the two traps ascend the next rise one close behind the other. Yonder the church can already be seen on its hillock, over the village fields. The number of vehicles grows, the church bells ring. . . .

A steamer has brought worshippers by another route, young summer visitors seized with the impulse to see the parish church and congregation. They have come by the lake-steamer, but have decided to return through the woods, by the path skirting the narrow waterway. . . . The church bells ring, a different rhythm now from that a moment ago, doubtless the parson's chime. . . . The congregation moves towards the doors; from the graveyard come those who had something to take there, a group apart for the moment, these. Farmhands from the neighbourhood and younger lads who seek their company mingle with the crowd and enter the church, or at least that part of it from which one can easily escape after a little while. The village cobbler, he with the hanging moustaches, a public character, known to be a leading spirit in the events of this summer, goes past the church with an expression of solemn indifference. He has been to the Post Office, on Union business.

Roses bloom on the overgrown graves; the sun heats the black silks of the farmers' wives until their cheeks glow and they try to pull down their silk shawls as low over their foreheads as the seemliness of the occasion will allow.

In church the air is cooler and moderately fresh; only faintly can a refined nose perceive the human smell characteristic of this people, imparted by successive generations to the interior of the church. The sound of fidgeting too is low, for there is less coughing in summer than in winter. Only the long spell of coughing of some old man is clearly heard, coughing that no longer depends on seasons, but is a reminder that the flame of life in the cougher is burning low and tends to splutter as it nears its extinction.

The organ quavers through a few runs of its own, pauses and bursts full-toned into the morning hymn, in which the congregation joins—the young people clearly and correctly, sure of the melody, the old people stumbling after as well as they can. Verse after verse of the hymn rolls out, until after the closing verse the organ does not stop, but hums gently a while, as though trying to withdraw its influence over the spirit of the congregation. The clergyman is at the altar.

The church is cruciform; on one side of the main aisle sit the women, on the other the men, facing the altar; on each side of the side aisles the worshippers face the main body of the church.

By the time the litany has well begun the mood of the congregation has become settled. A young gentleman, a stranger to the locality, gazes from the men's pews, next to the side aisle, at the congregation. Directly in front of him are the women, whom he can watch in profile, as with varying expressions they follow the altar service and respond in the litany. His gaze wanders, to be sure, hither and thither, among the women. For this feat he need not turn his head or attract attention to himself, nor do those he looks at observe him. But he has taken note, already during the morning hymn, of one worshipper and felt an emotional tremor pass through his being, an accidental encounter divined beforehand. The girl wears a simple headdress, a white summer kerchief knotted behind her head, so that the ends hang down to her shoulders. Under the edge of the kerchief, along her brow and temples, brown locks, whose glint already seems familiar, are visible; the face seen in profile is pure and devotional, the red of the mouth and curve of the upper lip giving it almost a child's expression.

She bows down now for the confession of sin, the words issuing in a solemn booming from the altar. One sees shoulders and bowed heads, clumsy and stiff, backs scarcely able to bend, worshippers straightening out to reveal the same immovable, frozen expressions as they wore when bowing down in confession, but the gaze of one man is fixed on a girl in the women's pews, and in the eyes of this man the girl's face appears to have become still purer than before during the confession, as though Sin itself in departing from her had left new beauty behind it. . . .

The light mood of the young man surrenders to the atmosphere of the sunlit church; the solemn rhythm of words and the organ hymns and amen-accompaniments, all uphold in his consciousness that one single picture, in which his sensitized faculties can see no blemish. The glances hitherto exchanged in everyday circumstances, even the sweet wordless playful struggle, recalled in this place to memory, were all prized fruits of life, honey held forth a single time and no more by life's dearest flower.

So, in the life of a clean young man, moments crystallise, like pearls from the generous hand of Life itself. They fall into the depths of the soul as an everlasting treasure, where, by those who have kept them clean, they are good to delight in afterwards. But there are many ways of keeping clean and of defiling; the same method may sometimes preserve, sometimes impair their purity.

Such is the church built and cultivated by Man during the morning of a fine summer Sunday. In the afternoon the devotional mood of the morning wears away as the Sunday itself. The fresh night draws nigh, when other paths are trod.

(Alexander Matson)

According to Sillanpää, nature and environment mold the man; he cannot evolve separately. The lives of his heroes are predestined; they are not guided by a cogitative faculty and a free, elective will. Silja, victimized by her fate at the age of twenty-two, serves as a poignant example. Sillanpää's study of natural science caused a biological bias in him. He delineated women with dignity, stressing their importance in the preservation of mankind. He analyzed the behavior of the young, the poor, the simple, the complex, and the neurotic.

 ## The Torchbearers

A few years after the proclamation of Finnish independence, the idea was conceived of promoting a cultural exchange with other nations. Literati, actors, musicians, philatelists, photographers, and other amateurs formed the organization *Nuoren Voiman Liitto* (League of Youth and Strength), which published its own journal, *Young Strength,* in 1924. In this same year, a group of young writers and poets founded the radical circle *Tulenkantajat* (the Torchbearers), and under this name published their newspaper from 1929–1930. The literary activity of this circle remained comparatively irrelevant; its primary task was to counteract the conservative ideology of the older generation. Its favorite slogan was "Open windows onto Europe." The group could get no substantial support from the public in general and failed to develop a noteworthy literary trend, for each of the associates represented a different inclination.

Of all the Torchbearers' poets, Uuno Kailas (1901–1933) was most prominent. Poverty, common to most writers of any small nation, and the strain of his creative work led to consumption and to his death at the age of thirty-two. Constant struggle and foreknown tragedy were the why and wherefore of his deep pessimism, his concern with ethical standards and his feelings of guilt:

The Guilty Man

He is being shot. He's the guilty man.
He is looking mutely at us and away from us.
He is now looking at me and commanding: Look!
And then I perceive who is also a guilty man.

The iron fetter of guilt encircles the wrists
Of all of us, all that my eyes can see;
Guilt's debtor slaves are we, and fettered to him,
And our consciences' armies lay siege to us.

But one of us that I see has broken death's fetter.
I see him doffing his dirty attire, I see
From the shade of guilt's wings how he enters the light.

I see his new face: he is the robber on the cross,
He's my brother, the guilty man, who is being shot.

(Cid Erik Tallqvist)

Professor Tarkiainen gives the following explanation: "But, though Kailas is facing death eye to eye, he does not deny that it is most exquisite in life to be a poet and as a poet to reveal eternal beauty."[11] Indeed, Uuno Kailas employed his talent to exalt the immaterial faculty of the soul.

The first poems of P. Mustapää (Martti Haavio, b. 1899) revealed national concerns that faded after World War II. Besides being a professor of folklore, Mustapää tried to link old-fashioned Finnish poetry with modern patterns. He com-

---

[11] Quoted by E. Saarinen in "Movements in Modern Finnish Literature," *The Norseman* XIV (July–Aug. 1956) 279.

posed six collections of poems; one of the more vivid and typical of these describes a tinsmith:

Dolce Far Niente[12]

The tin-smith Mr. Lindblad,
Outstretched as in a bed,
Is lying with a bushy
Grass tuft under his head;
And green is his bed cover—
Ho, hornets not your lover!
He's to his own thoughts wed.

He's a philosopher, Lindblad,
And he knows all about life;
He knows its two different aspects,
Its gentleness and its strife.
Grey grief he's had his measure
Sweet joy has given him pleasure,
With both his life was rife.

You fall asleep, then, Lindblad,
You drop your fragrant weed,
And so behind sleep's curtain
Thus softly you recede.
Yes, Lindblad, to retire
In dream-land to respire,
Is the philosopher's need.

(Cid Erik Tallqvist)

The woman lyric poet Katri Vala (Karin Alice Wadenström, 1901–1944), using a variety of pen names: Pekka, Viktoria, and Ilmarinen, published her first collections, *The Far Orchard* (1924) and *The Blue Door* (1926), during her affiliation with the Torchbearers. Katri Vala's contribution was twofold: she promoted modernism and confirmed free verse. As one of the founders of the progressive society *Kiila* ("the wedge," 1936), which was a more radical continuation of the Torchbearers,

---

[12] (Italian) sweet idleness.

the poetess worked tirelessly to promote leftist ideology among the masses, especially during political campaigns. Her left-wing political views and concurrent concern with social problems permeate *The Return* (1934) and *The Native Nest Is on Fire* (1942). Accused of being a communist, she went into exile in Sweden, where she died in 1945. Some of Katri Vala's poems are rather flamboyant:

Flowering Earth

The earth is teeming with the bluish-red clusters
    of the lilacs,
The flowering hoarfrost of the rowans,
    , The red star-clusters of the lime-worts.
Blue flowers, yellow flowers, white flowers
Are waving in the meadows as on senseless seas.
And the fragrance!
Sweeter than holy incense burning:
Hot and quivering and madly intoxicating
Pagan smell of the earth's skin.

To live, to live, to live!
To live frantically the supreme moment of life
With petals open to the utmost,
Live beautifully flowering,
Delirious with one's fragrance, with the sun—
Fully, intoxicatingly, to live!

What does it matter that death will come.
What does it matter that the multi-coloured love-
    liness
Will be scattered dried up on the earth,
Has it not flowered once!
Has not the sun shone,
Heaven's great and burning love,
Straight into the hearts of the flowers,
Even to the quivering core of their being.
                    (Cid Erik Tallqvist)

Mika Waltari (b. 1908) is the best known Finnish man of letters abroad. Several of his novels have been filmed in Hollywood. Neither the purpose of the Torchbearers nor the literary atmosphere of Paris, where he lived from 1927 to 1930, succeeded in making him modern; Waltari stubbornly kept his old-fashioned natural eloquence, invested all his energy in the building of a plot, and overshadowed all of the aforesaid members of the Torchbearers. He studied theology and philosophy at Helsinki University and has done considerable research. Critics say that his historical descriptions are accurate to the least detail.

While earning his living as a journalist, Waltari ventured into poetry with the religious lyric. During his stay in France he wrote *The Grand Illusion* (1928), a novel about the sentiments of youth, which gained him immediate recognition. His profitable novel *A Stranger came to Town* (1937) enabled him to dedicate his time exclusively to writing. Thus, he could record Finnish cultural and economic progress in the three-volume novel *From Father to Son* (1942), followed by the world-famous *The Egyptian* (1945). Dominating the foreground of this historical novel with his political and religious proceedings is the Pharaoh Amenhotep IV, who lived around 1300 B.C., and assumed the name of Ikhnaton. Egyptologists acclaim the authenticity of this re-creation in which the novelist perfectly combines research and imagination:

> The land under the sway of Babylon is called by many names; it is known as Chaldea and also the land of the Kassites after the people who live there. But I will call it Babylon, for everyone knows what land that is. It is a fertile country whose fields are threaded with irrigation ditches, and it is flat as far as the eye can see, differing from Egypt in this as in everything else. Thus, for example, while Egyptian women grind their corn in a kneeling position and turning a round stone, the women of Babylon sit and grind two stones together, which is of course more toilsome.
>
> There are so few trees that to fell one is regarded as an offense against gods and men and is punishable by law. But whoever plants a tree thereby wins the favor of the gods. The

inhabitants of Babylon are fatter and oilier than other people and like all fat folk are given to laughter. They eat heavy, floury food, and I saw a bird there they call a hen, which could not fly but lived among the people and laid an egg as large as a crocodile's egg for them every day, though no one hearing this would believe it. I was offered some of these eggs to eat, for the Babylonians regard them as a great delicacy, but I never ventured to try them and contented myself with dishes familiar to me or of which I knew the ingredients.

The people of the country told me that Babylon was the greatest and most ancient of all the cities in the world, though I did not believe them, knowing that Thebes is both the greatest and the oldest. There is no city in the world like Thebes, though I will admit that Babylon astonished me with its size and wealth. Its very walls were as high as hills and formidable to see, and the tower they had built to their gods soared to the sky. The town houses were four and five stories high so that people lived their lives above and below each other, and nowhere—not even in Thebes—have I seen such magnificent shops and such a wealth of merchandise as in the trading houses of the temple.

Their god was Marduk, and to the honor of Ishtar a gateway had been built that was loftier than the pylons of Ammon's temple. It was covered with many-colored glazed tiles fitted together into pictures that dazzled the eyes in sunlight. From this gateway a broad road ran to Marduk's tower, up which a spiral way led to the summit—a way so smooth and wide that a number of chariots might have been driven up it abreast. At the top of this tower dwelt the astrologers, who knew all the heavenly bodies, calculated their paths, and proclaimed auspicious and inauspicious days so that all might regulate their lives thereby. It was said they could foretell a man's destiny, though for this they had to know the day and hour of his birth. Being ignorant of my own, I could not put their science to the test.

I had as much gold as I cared to draw from the temple counting house, and I took up my dwelling near the Gate of Ishtar at a large inn many stories high, on the roof of which were gardens of fruit trees and myrtle bushes and where streams flowed and fish leaped in the pools. This inn was frequented by eminent people visiting Babylon from their country estates—if they had no town house of their own—and also by foreign envoys. The rooms were carpeted with thick mats and the couches soft with the skins of wild animals, while on the walls were frivolous pictures very gaily and colorfully pieced together with glazed tiles. This inn was called Ishtar's House of Joy and belonged, like all else of note in the city, to the Tower of the God.

Nowhere else in the world are so many different sorts of people to be seen or languages to be heard as in Babylon. The citizens say that all roads lead thither and that it is the center of the world. Its people are first and foremost merchants; nothing is more highly regarded than commerce, so that even their gods trade among themselves. For this reason they have no love for war, and they maintain mercenaries and build walls merely to safeguard their business. Their desire is for roads in every country to be kept open to all, chiefly because they know themselves to be the greatest merchants of any and that trade is of more advantage to them than war. Yet they are proud of the soldiers who guard their ramparts and temples and who march every day to the Gate of Ishtar, their helmets and breastplates gleaming with gold and silver. The hilts of their swords also and their spearheads are adorned with gold and silver in token of their wealth. They inquire eagerly of the stranger whether he has ever before seen such troops and such chariots.

The King of Babylon was a smooth-faced boy who had to hang a false beard on his chin when he mounted the throne. He loved playthings and strange tales. My fame had sped before me from Mitanni, so that when I put up at Ishtar's House of Joy and had spoken with the priests and doctors of the tower, I received word that the King commanded my attendance.

Kaptah as usual was anxious, and said to me, "Do not go, but rather let us fly together, for of kings no good thing can come."

But I said, "You fool, do you not remember that we have the scarab with us?"

"The scarab is the scarab," he rejoined, "and I have not

forgotten, but safety is better than hazard, and we must not try the scarab too high. If you are resolved to go, I cannot hinder you, and I will come, too, so that at least we may die together. But we must stand upon our dignity and request that a royal chair be sent to fetch us—and we will not go today, for by the custom of the country it is an evil day. The merchants have closed their shops, and the people rest in their houses and do no work. If they did, it would miscarry, this being the seventh day of the week."

I pondered this and knew that he was right. Though to Egyptians all days are alike, save those proclaimed unpropitious according to the stars, yet in this country the seventh day might be unlucky for an Egyptian also, and it was better to be prudent.

I said, therefore, to the King's servant, "You must take me for a simple foreigner indeed if you fancy I would appear before the King on such a day as this. Tomorrow I will come if your King will send a chair for me. I have no wish to come before him with dung between my toes."

The servant replied, "For these words of yours, Egyptian scum, I fear you will come before the King with a spear prodding your behind."

But he went and was certainly impressed, for the next day the King's chair came to Ishtar's House of Joy to fetch me. But the chair was a common one, such as is sent to bring tradesmen and other common people to the palace to show jewelry and feathers and apes.

Kaptah shouted loudly to the porters and to the runner, "In the name of Set and all devils! May Marduk scourge you with scorpions! Be off! As if it were seemly for my lord to travel in such a rickety old coop as that!"

The porters looked blank, and the runner threatened Kaptah with his staff. Onlookers began to gather at the inn door and laugh, saying, "In truth we long to see your lord for whom the King's chair is inadequate."

But Kaptah hired the great chair belonging to the inn, which required forty slaves to carry it; in this the ambassadors from powerful kingdoms went about their business, and in this also foreign gods were carried when they visited the city. And the bystanders laughed no longer when I came down from my room in a robe on which were embroidered in silver and gold the symbols of my calling. My collar glittered in the sunshine with gold and precious stones, while about my neck were hung chains of gold. The inn slaves followed with chests of cedarwood and ebony inlaid with ivory in which lay my medicines and my instruments. Indeed, there was no more laughing; rather, they bowed before me, saying one to another, "Truly this man must be as the lesser gods in wisdom. Let us follow him to the palace."

At the palace gates the guards dispersed the throng with their spears and raised their shields as a barrier, a very wall of gold and silver. Winged lions lined the way along which I was carried to the inner courts. Here an old man came to meet me whose chin was shaven after the fashion of scholars and in whose ears gleamed golden rings. His cheeks hung in discontented folds, and there was anger in his eyes as he addressed me.

"My liver is incensed because of the needless uproar you have caused by your arrival. The lord of the four quarters of the world is already asking what manner of man this is who comes when it suits him rather than when it suits the King— and who, when he does come, brings tumult with him."

I said to him, "Old man! Your speech is as the buzz of flies in my ear. Nevertheless, I ask who you may be to address me thus?"

"I am physician in chief to the lord of the four quarters of the world—and what swindler are you who come to entice gold and silver from the King? Know that if of his bounty he reward you with minted gold or silver, you must give half of it to me."

"I see that you would do better to talk to my servant, whose business it is to clear blackmailers and parasites from my path. Yet I shall be your friend since you are an old man and know no better. I shall give you these gold rings from my arm to show you that gold and silver are but as dust beneath my feet and that it is not for them that I have come but for wisdom."

I gave him the bracelets, and he was astonished and knew not what to say. He even allowed Kaptah to accompany me and brought us into the presence of the King.

King Burnaburiash sat on soft cushions in an airy room
with the walls glowing with brightly colored tiles, a spoiled,
sulky boy with his hand to his cheek. Beside him lay a lion
that growled softly as we appeared. The old man prostrated
himself to wipe the floor with his mouth before the King,
and Kaptah did the same. When he heard the growl, however, he bounced up on hands and feet like a frog with a yelp
of fear, which made the King burst out laughing and tumble
backward on his cushions, squirming with mirth. Kaptah
squatted on the floor, his hands raised defensively, while the
lion also sat up and yawned at great length, then clashed its
fangs together as the temple coffers close on a widow's mite.

The King laughed till the tears ran from his eyes. Then he
remembered his pain and moaned and put his hand to a
cheek so swollen that one eye was half closed. He scowled at
the old man, who hastened to say, "Here is that stubborn
Egyptian who would not come when you summoned him.
Say but the word, and the guards shall slit his liver."

But the King kicked at him, saying, "This is no time to
talk nonsense but for him to heal me at once. The pain is
terrible, and I fear that I may die since I have not slept for
many nights nor eaten anything but broth."

Then the old man lamented, striking his head against the
floor, "O lord of the four quarters of the world! We have
done all we might to heal you; we have offered jaws and
teeth in the temple to drive out the evil spirit that is lodged
in your jaw. More we have not been able to do because you
would not let us touch your sacred person. Nor do I think
this unclean Egyptian can do better than we."

But I said, "I am Sinuhe the Egyptian, He Who Is Alone,
Son of the Wild Ass, and I do not need to examine you to see
that a tooth has caused your cheek to swell because you did
not have it cleansed or drawn out in time as your physicians
must surely have counseled you to do. Such pains are for
children and the timid and not for the lord of the four quarters of the world, before whom the very lions tremble and
bow their heads as I see with my own eyes. Nevertheless, I
know your pain is great, and I will help you."

The King, still with his hand to his face, made answer,
"You speak boldly. Were I well, I should have your impru-

dent tongue cut out and your liver slit—but there is no time for that now. Cure me quickly, and your reward shall be great. But if you hurt me, I will have you slain without delay."

"Be it so. I have with me a small but remarkably powerful god, thanks to whom I did not come yesterday—for if I had, it would have been to no purpose. I can see that today the evil has ripened sufficiently for me to treat it, and this I shall do if you wish. But not even a king can the gods preserve from pain, though I declare to you that your relief when it is over will be so great that the pain will be forgotten and that I will make it as slight as any man in the world can make it."

The King hesitated for a while, scowling, with his hand to his cheek. He was a handsome boy when well, though spoiled, and I knew that I liked him. Feeling my eyes upon him, at last he said irritably, "What you have to do, do quickly."

The old man groaned and struck his head against the floor, but I paid him no heed. I ordered wine to be warmed, and with this I mixed a narcotic. He drank and after a time brightened a little, saying, "The pain is leaving me, and you need not plague me with your knives and forceps."

But my will was stronger. Tucking his head firmly into my armpit, I made him open his mouth, then lanced the boil on his jaw with a knife purified in the fire Kaptah had brought with him. The fire was not, indeed, the holy fire of Ammon; Kaptah had carelessly allowed this to go out on the journey down the river. The new flame Kaptah had kindled with a fire drill in my room at the inn, believing in his simplicity that the scarab was potent as Ammon.

The King uttered loud cries when he felt the knife, and the lion with blazing eyes rose up and roared, lashing its tail to and fro; but soon the boy was busily spitting. His relief was sweet, and I helped him by pressing lightly on his cheek. He spat, and wept for joy, and spat again, exclaiming, "Sinuhe the Egyptian, you are a blessed man although you hurt me." And he spat on unceasingly.

But the old man said, "I could have done that as well as he, and better, if only you had permitted me to touch your sacred jaw. And your dentist would have done it best of all."

He was astonished when I said, "This old man says truly, for he could have done it as well as I, and the dentist would have done it best. But their wills were not as strong as mine, and so they could not free you from your pain. For a physician must venture to cause pain even to a king when it is unavoidable, without fearing for himself. These feared, but I do not fear, for all is one to me, and your men are welcome to slit my liver when I have cured you."

The King spat and pressed his cheek, and the cheek was no longer painful.

"I never heard a man speak as you speak, Sinuhe. Truly you have brought me great relief; wherefore, I pardon you your insolence—and I forgive your servant also though he saw me with my head under your arm and heard me cry out. I forgive him because he made me laugh with his capering." To Kaptah he added, "Do it again!"

But Kaptah said wrathfully, "It is inconsistent with my dignity."

Burnaburiash said smiling, "We shall see."

He called the lion, and the lion rose and stretched till its joints cracked, its intelligent eyes upon its master. The King pointed to Kaptah, and the lion strolled lazily toward him waving his tail, while Kaptah drew back and back and gazed on the beast as if bewitched. Suddenly the lion opened its jaws and gave a muffled roar; Kaptah whipped about and, seizing the door hangings, scuttled up them and perched upon the lintel. He squeaked with terror as the animal dabbed up at him with its paw. The King laughed more than ever.

"Never did I see such clowning," he said.

The lion sat licking its chops while Kaptah clung to the lintel in great distress. But now the King ordered food and drink, declaring that he was hungry. The old man wept for joy that the King was cured, and many different foods were brought in on silver dishes, wine also in golden cups.

The King said, "Eat with me, Sinuhe! Ill though it befits my dignity, I will forget it today and not think of how you held my head under your arm and poked your fingers into my mouth."

So I ate and drank with him, and I told him, "Your pain is soothed, but may return at any time if the tooth that is the cause of it be not removed. Therefore, let the dentist draw it as soon as the swelling in your cheek has gone down, when it may be done without endangering your health."

His face darkened.

"You talk much and tediously, you crazy foreigner." Then after some reflection he added, "But it may be true, for the pain returns every autumn and spring when my feet are wet —and so badly that I wish I were dead. If it must be done then you shall do it, for I will not set eyes on that dentist again because of the needless pain he has caused me."

I answered him gravely, "Your dentist shall draw the tooth and not I, for in such matters he is the cleverest man in the country—cleverer also than myself—and I would not bring his anger upon my head. But if you wish it, I will stand beside you and hold your hands and encourage you while he does it, and I will soothe the pain with all the arts I have learned in many lands among many people. And this shall be done two weeks from today—for it is best to fix the time lest you repent of it. By then your jaw will be sufficiently healed, and meanwhile you shall rinse your mouth morning and evening with a remedy I shall give you, though it may sting and has an evil taste."

He grew angry. "And if I will not do this?"

"You must give me your sacred word that all shall be done as I have said—for indeed the lord of the four quarters of the world cannot go back upon that. And if you let it be done, I will divert you with my art and turn water into blood before your eyes—I will even teach you to do this and amaze your subjects. But you must promise never to reveal the secret to the priests of Ammon, and I should not know it myself were I not a priest of the first grade, nor dare to teach it to you were you not a king."

As I finished speaking, Kaptah cried out pitifully from the door frame, "Take away this devil's beast or I shall climb down and slay it, for my hands are numb and my backside sore with sitting in this uncomfortable place which in no way befits my dignity."

Burnaburiash laughed more than ever at this threat. Then feigning gravity he said, "It would indeed be a woeful thing if you killed my lion, for I have brought it up from a cub, and it is my friend. I will call it away, therefore, that you may not commit this evil deed in my palace."

He called the lion to him, and when Kaptah had climbed down the hangings, he stood rubbing his cramped legs and glaring at the lion so that the King laughed again and slapped his knees.

"A more comical man I never saw in my life. Sell him to me, and I will make you rich."

But I did not wish to sell Kaptah. The King did not insist, and we parted friends. He had begun to nod by now, and his eyelids were drooping, for he had had no sleep for many nights.

The old physician followed me out, and I said to him, "Let us take counsel together about what is to happen in two weeks' time, for that will be an evil day, and we should be wise to make sacrifice to all suitable gods."

This greatly pleased him, for he was a pious man, and we agreed to meet in the temple to make sacrifice and to confer with the doctors about the King's tooth. Before we left the palace, he caused refreshment to be offered to the porters who had brought me; they ate and drank in the forecourt and praised me volubly. They sang aloud as they carried me back to the inn, crowds followed us, and from that day my name was famous in Babylon. But Kaptah rode his white donkey in a great rage and would not speak to me, for he had been wounded in his dignity.

(Naomi Walford)

Other significant books by Waltari include *Michael the Finn* (1948), *The Sultan's Renegade* (1949), *The Dark Angel* (1952), *Moonscape* (1953), *The Etruscan* (1955), *Greetings from Finland* (1962). His novels, dramas, film scripts, and poetry comprise over forty volumes.

 Exploring Trends

Among writers of the younger generation the name of Väinö Linna (b. 1920) is popular. His chronicle *An Unknown Soldier* (1954), a dreary document on the Finno-Russian war of 1941–

1944, exploded into a bombshell reaching fifteen editions. Linna's trilogy, *Here, Under the North Star* (1959–1962), coldly and realistically describes the Civil War of 1918, its tragedy and irony, with an approach akin to Jaroslav Hašek's in *The Good Soldier Schweik*. Both works have been severely attacked by the Soviet Union. In his essays and reviews Väinö Linna defends the traditional form.

Poetry of great elegance is written by Elisabet Laurila, who has also produced short stories and novels. Her volumes of poems *The Sun Prairie* (1946), *The Sun Sets on the Mountain* (1950), and *The Panorama of Modern Lyrics* (1962) have been translated into several languages. The titles of her poems disclose a characteristic melancholy mood: "Alone," "Sad," "Waiting," "Loneliness," and "Evening Song." Impressive, beautiful, and smoothly-flowing poetry witnesses to Elisabet Laurila's skill, which was nurtured in her literary and esthetical studies at Helsinki University.

My Childhood Thought

When I was a child, I thought:
I will gather all great and beautiful thoughts
And give them to God.

Once older,
When life had stolen all affection and softness
      from my soul,
God, my Father, offered me absolution.

And every day
He sends into this searching heart
One clean, sweet thought from childhood.

      (Leo Vuosalo and Steve Stone)

Numerous nonsensical statements, devoid of logical connection and embodying ideas reminiscent of post-dadaism, strike the reader in the volumes of poetry written by Pentti Saarikoski (b. 1927): *Poems* (1957), *Other Poems* (1958), *My Poems and the Poems of Hipponax* (1959), *About the World* (1961), and

Pope and Tsar (1962). Saarikoski rebelled against his father, the social order, and Christianity. The poet says that he became a communist to realize his desires.[13] He expresses cynism and scorn:

Poem, from "Greek Sequence"

Life was given to man
for him to consider
in which position
he wants to be dead:

Grey skies float by,
star-meadows hang

and the earth
comes into your mouth
like bread.
                    (Anselm Hollo)

An infatuation for experiment and a somewhat vague philosophy characterize the collections of Paavo Haaviko (b. 1931): *The Distant Ways* (1951), *In the Windy Nights* (1953), *The Land of Birth* (1955). A case in point is the following extract from *The Winter Palace* (1959):

I want poetry to have only the faintest smell.
I think I am an object, as hopeful as the grass.
These likes are improbable, as this
is a journey through known speech
toward the region that is nowhere.
                    (Anselm Hollo)

In the miniature novel *The Years* (1962), Haaviko unmasks the stereotyped conflicts which cause Väinö to ruin his family and to become an alcoholic.

---

[13] See his article "I am a Writer—I am a Communist" in the *International P.E.N.*, I (1965), 25–26.

Estonian Literature

Folklore

The ancient Estonians had their songs, myths, and tales prior to the birth of Christ. The majority of them were rather original; some were identical with those of other Finno-Ugric nations. Many of these oral traditions failed to survive because of their primitivism and archaic expressions. Only in the nineteenth century did Rev. Jakob Hurt (1839–1907), the so-called King of Folklore, urge the nation to collect its oral literature. The National Archives of Folklore has registered 370,000 songs, about 100,000 fairy tales, 160,000 sayings and proverbs, and 90,000 riddles. Among these are legends explaining the origin of hills, lakes, and rivers. Humorous and ironic tales generally treat foreign invaders. The animal stories correspond to typical geographical locations and are often based on the theme of justice:

The Wolf and the Reindeer

A lofty reindeer was strolling through the forest. Suddenly he heard someone crying for help. He followed the sound and noticed that a giant fir broken by the wind had pinioned a wolf beneath its weight.

The reindeer shook his head and asked:

"How could such a misfortune befall you, my neighbor?"

"There is no time for inquiries, dear friend. My death may come any minute. Hurry to lift the windfall with your mighty horns."

"It will be my honor to rescue you."

The reindeer exerted all his strength, lifted the heavy timber carefully and held it until the wolf crawled out. Then the rescuer shook his head proudly and continued his journey.

"Don't move!" the wolf commanded.

"Why not?"

"I want to eat you!"

"But I have saved your life!"

"It doesn't matter!"

They argued for a long time, until the reindeer suggested:
"Let's consult someone else. Perhaps he can tell who is right and who is wrong."

"All right," the wolf agreed.

They wandered about the woods and, finally, met a bear. He listened to the complaints of both disputants, thought for a while, and pronounced:

"I cannot pass judgment without a proper investigation. We must go to the place of the incident."

The wolf and the reindeer agreed, and all three of them set out for the examination. The bear poked around the windfall clumsily, contemplated longer than before, and stated:

"I must see how it happened. Reindeer, do you expect me to believe that you really could lift this huge tree?"

"Of course, brother bear," he exclaimed joyfully and placed the trunk on his horns.

"Wolf," the bear said, "show me whether you are able to hide in these branches."

"I shall feel comfortable there," the wolf replied and jumped to his previous position.

"Release the windfall!" the bear commanded.

The reindeer dropped the fir trunk, and the wolf found himself in the trap. He was there before, and he is there again. And who would have mercy on an evil and greedy wolf?

(Aleksis Rubulis)

International themes dominate tales dealing with ghosts, sprites, werewolves, treasure troves, and witchcraft. In mythological tales, superstitions have mingled with Christian traditions. All of them depict traits peculiar to the northern nature, as illustrated in "The Milky Way":

When the world was ready for population, God created a beautiful girl and put her in charge of all the birds. Her name was Linda, the daughter of Uku.[1] Linda cared for the birds like a mother, and all of the singing creatures loved her. A throng of suitors desired her for a wife.

[1] Uku or Ukko is a principal mythological god of the Estonians and Finns. Occasionally he appears as a water god, sometimes evil.

Once, the North Star[2] arrived in an icy coach drawn by six grey steeds and offered her ten presents. "Go back," Linda replied, "and stay on the guard you have neglected."

Soon, the Moon approached in a silver coach drawn by ten brown steeds, and brought twenty presents. "You always travel one and the same road, but change yourself constantly," said the girl as she rejected her admirer.

The Sun didn't hesitate, either. He descended in a golden coach drawn by twenty red steeds, and delivered thirty presents. However, Linda answered, "I don't love you. Your work is similar to that of the Moon; you are simply running on the same course."

The Northern Light came in a diamond coach drawn by a thousand white steeds. He ordered his servants to unload gifts of gold, diamonds, pearls, and assorted jewelry. The wooer pleased Linda, and she said, "You differ from the others, because you have a will of your own. You do what pleases you, and you rest whenever you wish. You live in splendor and magnificence, bedecking yourself in varied attire. I accept your proposal with joy."

But the North Star, the Moon, and the Sun showed their envy. When the Northern Light had to return to his duty at midnight, he promised to marry Linda as soon as possible and to take her to the North. He delayed, however, and the bride waited in vain. She grieved and wept for her beloved. Dressed in a bridal gown, she sat, one morning, on the bank of a river and burst into tears with such vehemence that brooks rose and rippled forth. Great flocks of birds circled to comfort their mistress, but she remained oblivious of them.

Finally, the sad news reached Uku. He commanded the wind to bring his daughter to heaven, where she now lives. Anyone who glances at the Milky Way may recognize her bridal veil beset with sparkling diamonds. She has forgotten all sorrow and still directs the birds on their difficult migrations. From time to time Linda waves her hand, sending regards to the Northern Light. Every winter the Northern Light visits his bride and perseveres in courting her. But

[2] In the Finno-Ugric folklore the sun, planets, and stars are considered male deities.

Uku strictly insists that his daughter remain in heaven permanently. The Milky Way will, therefore, last forever.

(Aleksis Rubulis)

Estonian folklore has played a relatively insignificant role in the development of modern literature. Encouraged by the *Kalevala,* Friedrich Robert Fählmann (1798–1850) and Friedrich Reinhold Kreutzwald (1803–1882) discovered great value in the oral works. Assuming that, centuries ago, Estonians must have had a national epic, both physicians decided to reconstruct the lost work. Fählmann died soon afterwards, leaving only a sketch. In 1851, the Estonian Learned Society entrusted the completion of the task to Kreutzwald. For over thirty years he collected ancient legends, myths, and songs, obtaining an abundance of material. Each genuine verse and prose fragment contained an allegoric trace of Estonian history and culture in a fragmentary arrangement. To achieve a uniform composition, the compiler merged these fragments into a composite whole by means of his own versification, which he based on folk poetry. Kreutzwald named his *magnum opus,* the *Kalevipoeg* [The son of Kalev]. In its final edition it was published, together with a German translation, by the Estonian Learned Society in 1857–1861. The epic comprises 18,993 verses and is divided into twenty songs. Following is a summary of the plot:

SONG 1.   Three brothers set out in different directions: one settled in Russia and became a merchant; another reached Lapland and became a warrior; the third, Kalev (the father of heroes), arrived in Estonia on an eagle and founded a kingdom. In one of his provinces lived a young widow who found a hen, an egg of a grouse, and a crow. The hen grew into the fair maiden Salme, the egg gave birth to another maiden, Linda, but the crow became an orphan girl. Beautiful Salme, who had many suitors, chose the Youth of the Stars. Linda, rejecting five other wooers, accepted the handsome giant Kalev. Their wedding was celebrated throughout Estonia.

SONG 2.   The royal couple lived happily and had several sons. When Kalev grew old, he chose his yet unborn son, Kalevid, as successor and predicted great fortune and glory for him. Linda called upon the Moon, the Evening Star, and the Sun to assist her sick husband but in vain. After his death, Linda wept for seven days and nights without eating and sleeping. She piled a hill of rocks upon his grave, over which the Cathedral of Tallinn was built. Soon the son was born. Various suitors pestered the queen, but she rejected them all. Her last admirer, the famous wind-magician from Finland, promised his revenge.

SONG 3. Aike[3] was crossing the iron bridges of the sky in his brazen chariot. He thundered, the wheels emitted sparks, from his right hand lightning struck into the horde of evil demons seeking refuge in the sea. Kalevid dragged them out like crabs on the rocks, helping Aike destroy them. Then three princes, including Kalevid, set out hunting with three dogs. They killed a bear, a bull, an elk, five dozen wolves, foxes, and hares. The younger brother carried the booty home by himself. Meanwhile, the Finnish sorcerer had kidnapped their mother, Linda. When she called for help, Pikker struck down the Sorcerer with lightning. The queen attempted to escape, but the gods transformed her into a rock, releasing her from affliction. The brothers searched for their mother in vain. Kalevid then consulted his father at the grave.

SONG 4. Kalevid plunged into the sea and swam toward Finland. The hero met a brown-eyed girl on an island and seduced her. Alarmed by his daughter's cry, her father arrived armed with a heavy club. He trembled, however, when he saw the titan, whom he considered a god. The girl fell from a cliff into the sea. Kalevid, unsuccessful in rescuing her, continued his journey northward. The parents combed the sea with both net and rake, but they detected nothing more than an oak, a fir, a silver dish, and similar objects. Out of the depth of the sea a copper man raised his voice in song, depicting the girl's destiny.

SONG 5. While in Finland, Kalevid uprooted an oak, fashioned a club out of it, and approached the sorcerer for revenge. The latter produced masses of warriors who swarmed upon

[3] Aike, often called Pikker or Pikne, is the mythological Estonian god of thunder, who fights demons.

Kalevid. But the giant crushed them all with his flailing club and killed the sorcerer.

Song 6. Kalevid purchased a gigantic sword, already bespoken by his late father, from a famous smith. The price of the sword was his participation in a fetching contest at a seven-day drinking bout. Affected by beer and mead, the hero revealed his experience on the island. The eldest son of the smith cast aspersion on him until Kalevid, enraged, struck off his head. The smith cursed the giant and his new sword.

The oak, which the islanders pulled out of the sea and planted, grew into the sky nearly reaching the sun. When a dwarf started to hew the tree, he turned into a giant. Within three days the oak was felled, and its trunk served as a bridge from Estonia to Finland across the island.

Song 7. Kalevid returned to Estonia sincerely repentant for both of his offenses. The brothers discussed who should rule the kingdom, but they couldn't agree and the decision was postponed. Kalevid visited his father's grave once more and received comfort from him.

Song 8. The brothers agreed that strength and mastery at a stone-throwing competition should determine a successor to the throne. The eldest brother flung his rock into the middle of the chosen lake. The second brother's stone landed on the opposite shore near the lake, splashing the mud. The youngest brother hurled his rock beyond the lake onto firm ground and won the contest. His brothers amiably left the kingdom. Kalevid, however, was troubled, for he now had to accept the responsibilities of governing the country.

Song 9. Messengers informed Kalevid that enemy troops were ravaging Estonia. Ukko appeared in a vision and instructed the king to save the innocent people. Kalevid ordered warriors dispatched for the defense of his kingdom.

Song 10. Two demons quarreled over the apportionment of a swamp.[4] Kalevid appointed his relative Alevid to settle the argument. Alevid outwitted the demons and took all their

[4] According to Estonian, Latvian, and Lithuanian superstitions, demons and devils live in swamps.

treasure. Kalevid and one of the demons engaged in a contest. The demon grabbed a rock the size of a sauna and hurled it on the very shore of Lake Virts. Kalevid's rock landed at Lake Peipsi. As soon as the wrestling match started, the king seized the demon and threw him toward the sky. When the demon reached the ground, he rolled for seven miles and lay unconscious for seven days. But the king made up his mind to build cities and to fortify them. On his trip to Lake Peipsi, Kalevid met the Air-Maiden, daughter of the Thunder-God, who grieved over dropping her ring into a well. Soon Kalevid emerged with a millstone on his finger and presented it to the girl.

Song 11. A sorcerer observed Kalevid wading through Lake Peipsi and carrying over twenty dozen heavy planks to build homes for his people. When the titan was resting, the sorcerer stole his sword and accidentally dropped it deep into the mud of the river Käpä. Responding to the call of its master, the sword replied that it lay among beautiful mermaids. It also reminded him of the murder of the smith's favorite son. Kalevid consented to its repose and ordered it to cut off the feet of the man who had brought the sword there if he should cross the river. The king referred, of course, to the sorcerer but unwittingly implicated himself.

Song 12. Three sons of the sorcerer assaulted Kalevid, but he defeated all of them with the planks and with a club thirty-five ells long. The angry sorcerer cast a spell over the hero, who fell asleep for seven weeks, dreamed of a new magic sword, and experienced a nightmare.

Song 13. While marching home, Kalevid entered a cave of demons. He freed three sisters from captivity and noticed the sword he had seen in his dream.

Song 14. The following day Kalevid inspected the underworld palace. Soon Sarvik[5] arrived. Kalevid defeated him in a wrestling match, seized his treasure, put the sisters and the planks on his shoulders, and rushed home.

---

[5] Literally, "Hornie"; ruler of the underground.

SONG 15. Tühi[6] and seventy other demons pursued the fugitives. A flood, created by a wishing rod of the youngest sister, separated them. Kalevid answered the questions of Tühi ironically and boastfully. All of the sisters married kinsmen of Kalevid.

SONG 16. Kalevid decided to investigate the edge of the world, where the earth and the sky come together. He made a boat, *Lennuk*,[7] of silver, secured gold armor, and set out in the course of the Great Bear with a large crew and wise men. One of his helmsmen spoke the languages of all nations, beasts, and birds. When Kalevid towed his vessel to a strange shore, the birds informed him that he had landed in Lapland. The king hired Varrak[8] to pilot the ship farther. They visited the Island of Fire,[9] which was filled with flames, smoke, and boiling water. In the next country a little daughter of a giant carried all of them to her father in an apron. The giant released them, after testing their wisdom by three puzzles. Afterwards the explorers met beings, half human and half dog, with long tails.[10] A fight broke out, but peace was soon restored. Kalevid gave the command to sail homeward.

SONG 17. Many fortified cities arose in Estonia, the greatest of which was Lindanisa,[11] built by Olev.[12] At this time enemy forces were invading the land. The king gathered his troops and crushed the aggressor. Sarvik appeared under the guise of a dwarf, but Kalevid hurled him into the ground by giving him a fillip.

SONG 18. Kalevid was determined to descend into hell. He surmounted many obstacles with the advice of a raven, a mouse, a toad, a cricket, and a crayfish. A fierce battle broke out between the giant and the hosts of hell at the iron bridge span-

[6] One of the principal demons.

[7] Literally, airplane.

[8] A Lapp.

[9] Perhaps Iceland.

[10] According to Baring-Gould, they must have been Eskimos in Greenland.

[11] "The Bosom of Linda," named by Kalevid in memory of his mother; now Tallinn, capital of Estonia.

[12] Kalevid's cousin and a famous builder, appointed by Kalevid.

ning the river of burning pitch. The victorious hero gained entrance to the main hall and started a dispute with Sarvik.

SONG 19. After a week of struggle Kalevid chained Sarvik to a rock, took his treasure, and departed to Lindanisa. During the celebration of a great feast, a Latvian and Polish attack[13] was announced. Varrak decided to return to Lapland and chose for his award the late Kalev's book of wisdom, which had an iron cover and was chained to a wall. The king agreed, for he couldn't read. Once more Kalevid visited his father's grave.

SONG 20. The son of Kalev hid his treasure and cast a spell over it. The shrill sound of his horn resounded all over Estonia, summoning its sons to defend their country. The massacre began. Innumerable corpses from the ranks of both adversaries dotted the battlefield, and no charms could stop the bleeding of the wounded. After gaining a temporary victory, the Estonians buried their fallen heroes in three days. Another engagement lasted for seven days. Dead bodies of the enemy, clad in mail, lay a fathom deep in blood. Unable to endure this any longer, Kalevid entrusted his kingdom to Olev. The son of Kalev withdrew into the woods and built himself a cottage on the river Koiva where he lived as a hermit.

Because strangers often intruded, the retired king decided to move to Lake Peipsi. But when Kalevid started to cross the river Käpä, his own sword instantly cut off both his feet.[14] The giant ascended into heaven, where he listened to the songs of his heroic deeds. Then the gods ordered Kalevid to guard Sarvik at the gates of Põrgu,[15] chaining his own hand to a rock. However, someday a fire will melt the rock and then Kalevid will free himself and restore happiness to Estonia.

In his lecture at the Estonian Learned Society in 1839, G. Schultz-Bertrams declared: "Let's give the nation an epic and a history; the rest will be won." Perhaps this was the reason why Kreutzwald used only those stories which best extol Kalevi-

---

[13] Apparently confused with the knights of the Teutonic Order.

[14] According to some tales, his legs were cut off by the enemy soldiers. Only then did his sword fall into the river.

[15] Hell.

poeg's heroism, courage, dedication, and similar virtues. However, the hero also has negative qualities. He is boastful, cruel to a certain extent, and deserts his country at the time of its greatest need.

Although Kreutzwald had studied Goethe's *Faust* and Lönnrot's *Kalevala* and had gained experience writing poems and didactic stories, his epic lacks unity. The author's rhetorical verses are scarcely in harmony with the genuine folklore. For about forty years this heroic epic was second only to the Bible and advanced Estonian culture and national pride.

 The Age of Enlightenment

During the time of the Iron Age (800 B.C.–100 A.D.), Estonia was independent and its inhabitants were occupied primarily with hunting, fishing, agriculture, and cattle-breeding. While the ancient Estonians possessed all the basic tools, were skilled in handicraft, and had commercial relations with the Goths, Germans, Danes, and other nations, until the thirteenth century they were acquainted with oral literature only. At that time the Teutonic knights of Germany reduced the people to serfdom. However, they also brought Christianity, fortified the already existing Western culture in the area, and introduced literacy. Thus, separate Estonian words and some phrases appeared in print in Heinricus de Lettis' *Heinrici Chronicon Lyvoniae* (1225). Two clergymen, Johann Köll and Simon Wanradt, wrote the *Short Catechism* (1535), believed to be Estonia's first book. After 1625, Gustavus II, king of Sweden, ruled over Estonia. He introduced many reforms, supported the foundation of Tartu University (1632), a teachers' college, and two high schools. Several religious books were published. The first Estonian grammar, Heinrich Stahl's *Anführung zu der Ehstnischen Sprach,* was issued in 1637. The great Northern War (1700–1721) delayed the translation of the Bible until 1739. According to the Treaty of Nystad (1721), the devastated Estonian terrain fell under Russian control. Conditions worsened, and works circulated solely in manuscript form. At this time, with the help of clergy and laymen educated in the previously established institutions, West-European ideas had sufficiently penetrated the subdued nation to bring about the literary enlightenment.

Kreutzwald's epic has played a twofold role: first, it instigated productive activity among Estonian writers and poets; secondly, it aroused national pride. In 1857 Johann Woldemar Jannsen (1819–1890), a teacher, issued the first Estonian weekly, *The Postman of Pärnu*. In 1864, he moved the paper, renamed *The Estonian Postman*, to Tartu, a center of activity for the Estonian Learned Society, which had been founded in 1838. The newspaper proved to be an invaluable instrument of communication among the intelligentsia and the people in general.

The patriotic fervor and the literary activity of Lydia Koidula (1843–1886) were the result, to a large extent, of both the *Kalevipoeg* and the press. As Jannsen's daughter, she assisted her father in editing *The Postman of Pärnu* and *The Estonian Postman*. A leading poet of her period, she began her career by adapting German works, e.g., her first collection of verses, *Meadow Flowers* (1866). Her original poetry appeared in the volume *The Nightingale of the Emajōgi*[16] (1866), in which patriotic motifs predominate. Lydia Koidula also wrote the first Estonian comedy, *What a Mulk* (1872), which focuses upon differences among peasants. Many of her poems were converted into popular songs. The poetess suffered greatly when, in 1873, she was forced to leave Estonia and take up permanent residence in Kronstadt, where her German-Latvian husband, Eduard Michelson, worked as a doctor at the Russian naval base.

Friedrich Kuhlbars (1841–1924) continued Lydia Koidula's tradition. He borrowed heavily from the *Kalevipoeg* for his collection of romantic poems *Wanemuine* (1870). A follower of the same trend was the linguist Mihkel Weske (1843–1890), but his collected works, *Dr. Weske's Songs* (1899), express more

---

[16] The largest river in Estonia, which empties into Lake Peipsi.

optimism. Influenced by Ivan Krylov, in *Awaken Voices* (1892) Jakob Tamm (1861–1907) presented mystic ballads and fables. Karl Eduard Sööt (1862–1950) was a more productive poet. In the two-volume *Meadow Blossoms* (1890–1891), the theme of nationalism mingles with that of love. The poet's personal experiences are portrayed in *Delight and Sorrow* (1894), while *The Fate* (1899) contains mostly melancholy verses about his deceased mother. A variety of motifs are included in *Reminiscences and Hopes* (1903), *The Home* (1921), and *The Childhood Paradise* (1923). His last book, *Crescent* (1937), contains some ballads. The creator of the Estonian love lyric, Anna Haava (1864–1957), experimented with free verse in her first three volumes, all entitled *Poems* (1888, 1890, 1897). Contemporary topics dominate *The Waves* (1906), *Cross-Waves* (1910), *Children of the North* (1913), *From Our Days* (1920), *The Life Still Is Beautiful* (1930), and *I Sing My Estonian Song* (1935). Her short stories are collected in *Small Portrayals from Estonia* (1911).

 Realism

Serfdom was abolished in Northern Estonia in 1816 and in Southern Estonia in 1819. Peasants were granted freedom of movement and choice of profession, but they remained without land. They had to rent plots from the manor lords and provide compensation with their labor. Several peasant revolts arose in the middle of the nineteenth century, and by the end of the century peasants were allowed to purchase land or to lease it on long-term contracts. The press increased publications of West-European literature, particularly German and French. However, Russification was intensified, and, through strict censorship, every work of poetry and prose based on Estonian history was suppressed. Estonian men of letters then realized that the time had come to treat contemporary topics from a more practical and effective aspect.

Eduard Vilde (1865–1933) wrote his first story, "On the

Evil Path" (1882), at the age of seventeen. He began his career working as a journalist for the newspapers of Tallinn, Tartu, Riga, and Berlin, but later he became the first Estonian professional literary writer. In Berlin in 1890–1892 he became acquainted with works of G. Hauptmann, Zola, Balzac, Sudermann, Ibsen, and other naturalists and realists. As the result of this, in his own realistic novel *A Cup Full of Poison* (1893) the young writer attempted to describe miserable living conditions of the poor. The next realistic novel, *To the Cold Country* (1896), demonstrates Vilde's increased maturity in his portrayal of the hero, who becomes a thief, the victim of his environment. Vilde is also the author of a historical trilogy, the first volume of which, *The War at Mahtra* (1902), deals with the peasant uprising; the second, *When the Peasants of Anija Visited Tallinn* (1903), describes mainly the lives of the nobility and the artisans, while the third, *The Prophet Maltsvet* (1906), speaks of emigration and disappointment.

Because of Vilde's participation in the 1905 revolution, he was forced to escape to Finland. There he continued his political ideology in his own satirical journal, *The Pillory* (1906). His travels then led him to Germany, Denmark, and the United States. A volume of his stories, *The Grin,* appeared in Estonia in 1913. Vilde's novel *The Dairyman of Mäeküla* (1916) delineates a wealthy lord who maintains an intimate relationship with the wife of a dairyman he employs. This triangle ends in tragedy and the dairyman's death. The artistic value of the work lies in Vilde's characterization and his handling of psychological conflict. In 1917 Vilde returned to Estonia, where he prepared the thirty-three volumes of his *Collected Works* for publication (1923–1935).

Juhan Liiv (1864–1913) showed promising talent in his first poems, published in 1885. Although he had become mentally ill by 1893, he continued writing during his lucid intervals. He found a publisher for only one volume of his poetry, *Poems* (1909), while hundreds of other poems were scattered in the press and periodicals. From time to time, the poet exhibited flashes of optimism characterized by his violations of meter and rhyme, but the majority of his works correspond to his misfortune: there are sombre pictures of his own personality, of autumn, dark woods, snow, frost, and withered flowers. Liiv also dedicated songs to his unfortunate fatherland, of which he speaks with equal melancholy but with sincere respect and love, e.g., "I Would Take a Garland of Flowers":

> I would take a garland of flowers
> And bind you with its mirth,
> And furl you in its fragrance,
> Estonia's orphaned earth.
>
> I would take the azure of heaven,
> And the brilliance of risen light,
> And the colours of dawn and setting,
> And crown you in all men's sight.
>
> I would take the bands of affection,
> Of honour and loyalty,
> And fold you in their comfort
> To still your agony.
>
> I would take blood's sacred meshes
> And the strong heart's every strand,
> And brace you with their valour,
> Unfortunate Motherland.
>
> (W. K. Matthews)

Discord among his own compatriots grieved Juhan Liiv most. He was aware of his illness; he realized that his poems were eccentric and, therefore, destroyed many of them. Occasionally his expression is naturalistic and resembles folk poetry, but first of all he is a symbolist. A more constant realism predominates in collections of his short stories, *Ten Stories* (1893), *The Cuckoo from Käkimägi* (1893), *The Curtain* (1894), *The Daughter of the Sorcerer* (1895), and in the volume of miniatures *From the Depth of the Life* (1909).

Playwright August Kitzberg (1856–1927) started his career

by publishing a number of rustic tales. After writing didactic plays, such as *Punga-Mart and Uba-Kaarel* (1892) in which he unequivocally attacked drinking, Kitzberg created an outstanding tragedy based on superstition, *The Werewolf* (1912). In the naturalistic drama *God Mammon* (1915) the avaricious hero neglects his family and forgets friends. The comedy *The Cursed Farm* (1923) points to the fact that Estonians had educated young men; the administration, however, failed to provide them with proper jobs.

Ernst Särgava (1868–1958) also belongs to the realistic trend. His short stories employ barbed irony to criticize the nobility for social injustice. In the novel *Instructor of the People* (1904), Särgava depicts a teacher, Madar, who came to the town of Mudila as an idealist, but, too weak to resist his environment, he becomes just another timeserver. Särgava's dialogues are vivid; his description is heavily satirical.

Jakob Mändmets (1871–1930) is known for his village stories in the collections *Stories of the Night-herdsmen* (1901), *The Pastor Römer* (1917), and *Through the Underwood* (1927). Although his style lacks originality, his structure and the psychological entanglements which he depicts contain a certain power. In *The Sea* (1914) and *Gust on the Reef* (1921) Mändmets treats the sea as a supernatural phenomenon.

 Neoromanticism

When tsarist troops ruthlessly crushed the 1905 revolution, several Estonian writers sought refuge in Finland, Germany, and France, where they acquired knowledge of contemporary literary movements and schools. Poet Gustav Suits beckoned: "We want more culture! More European culture! Let us remain Estonians, but let us also become Europeans!" Several smaller revolts emerged, and Nicholas II proved as inefficient as ever in controlling his empire. The occupied minorities did their utmost to exploit the situation. More and more young people were allowed to enroll in educational institutions. Censorship relaxed. The theater "Vanemuine" was established in Tartu (1906) and "Estonia" in Tallinn (1913). The National Museum became a cultural and political center. In 1905 the literary movement *Noor-Eesti* (Young Estonia) was founded.

The poet, and later professor of Estonian literature at Tartu University, Gustav Suits (1883–1956) was the chief representative of Young Estonia. He possessed both a thorough knowledge and a habit of self-criticism. Already in his first volume of poetry, *The Fire of Life* (1905), Suits displayed a certain maturity. He also replaced the popular four-verse stanza with a greater variety of stanza-forms. The 1905 revolution drove him to Finland, where he studied the humanities at Helsinki University. Later he moved to Sweden. "My Island," taken from the aforementioned volume, marks the beginning of the poet's restlessness:

> Still I keep sailing and sailing,
> And seeking an isle in the sea:
> I have sought it long already
> Where the random winds sail free.
>
> The sea has many islands
> And havens expectant with light,
> But I cannot find the island
> I dreamed in the dazzled night.
>
> And still my vessel keeps scudding
> On a swaying circular plain,
> And the clouds above me go swaying,
> And I seek my island in vain.
>
> (W. K. Matthews)

His next volume, *The Land of Winds* (1913), is divided into four cycles in which the poet describes his lost native land during the four seasons of the year. By this time his technique has improved, and his style is somewhat musical. The poet's youthful enthusiasm has vanished entirely. Although Suits maintained close contact with his friends in Estonia, he was constantly pensive and melancholy, as is clearly indicated in the poem "Buried in the Wind":

> All my songs I sing are changed,
> set to the tune of shady time.
>
> Times come and go but I keep singing
> while billows swell in raging storms.
>
> The wheel of life rolls ever farther,
> my song and I sway buried in the wind.
>   (Aleksis Rubulis)

The book *All Is But a Dream* (1922) adds revolutionary topics. It is heavy with solitude but depicts some courage:

All Is But a Dream

> I, mute exile, walk through showering
>   Leaves in towering
> Forest halls. The year is dead.
> Naked aspens. Wilted bracken.
>   Branches blacken
> Against skies of smouldering red.
>
> There, above, the bright-domed fastness
>   Of heaven's vastness,
> Here the kingdom of decay.
> Wind-swept fir-trees sing like soughing
>   Organs—bowing,
> Meeting treetops swing and sway.
>
> In this music all our jaded
>   Thought seems faded,
> Life's great core appears, sublime:
> Flames of heaven whose radiance blazes
>   Through our hazes,
> Infinite, like space and time.

Though this life, this struggling, milling
   Fight and killing
Weigh us down with grief and care:
All this earth is but illusion,
   Its confusion
A mere dream that rests on air.

Empty air bears all this savage
   Hate and ravage.
All this grim intensity
Circles round the sun, this grinning
   Lust keeps spinning,
Hurled through deep immensity.

Mortal seed—a shoot emerges,
   Driven by urges
Of eternal, changeless change:
Ah, behold the evening's boundless
   Glow, with soundless
Voices calling, vast and strange!

Through the leafless trees' dark quiver,
   Boughs that shiver,
See its line of endless light!
Though some cloudy monster cross it,
   Winds will toss it
Off its course in headlong flight.

Shadows lengthen, all seems dimmer,
   Pinetops glimmer
On high hills, but night comes soon,
Eastwards, cool and luminescent,
   See the crescent
Of the slowly rising moon.

Through the moonlight's silver hazes
   Memory raises
Shapes, forgotten and forlorn,
Beckoning shapes, while on the lonely

Crossroads only
Clamouring nightwinds moan and mourn.

Did a wing beat? Footsteps hustle?
      Only rustle
Of tall forests fills the night.
In their swelling voice, their soaring,
      Solemn roaring
Die all cries of crime and fright.

And my soul that strained and languished,
      Hurt and anguished,
Prays. Its silent words are these:
Watchman, watch the voiceless traitors,
      Desecrators,
The invisible disease!

Justice, raise thy heavy hammer—
      Hear the clamour
Of torn hearts, of griefs that gnaw
At torn nations, send thy frightening
      Sheets of lightning—
Judge the judge of lawless law!

Hours of evening, spent in turning
      Eyes to burning
Lights of heaven, are my prayer.
Now I go, as evening dwindles,
      But night kindles
Stars—they sparkle everywhere.

Distant worlds, my glances reach you:
      I beseech you,
Let my searching soul aspire
Through the endless depth it faces,
      Starry spaces,
To your gardens of desire!

Yet a chilling whisper shakes me
      And awakes me:

Fool, you trust your vision's lure!
Against Evil's cunning courses
   Join your forces,
Fight it, all whose hearts are pure!

See the city, see it blazon
   Forth its brazen
Pride—you, dreamer of bright stars,
Take the challenge through its glaring
   Streets, its blaring,
Drunken noise, its whirl of cars!

Dazzling haunts' rank turmoil thickens,
   Malice quickens.
Here, where fortune scars the soul,
Where all sanctity has vanished,
   Hoard the banished
Longings—guard the glowing coal!

                                  (Ants Oras)

Gustav Suits' last volume, *Flames in the Wind* (1950), reflects his lifelong recollections and was published when he once again lived as an exile in Sweden. Because of Suits' mastery of form and style, his works still serve as models for many young poets.

Friedebert Tuglas (b. 1886) is considered a leading prose writer of the Young Estonia school. A member of the Social Democrat Party, from 1906 until 1917 he lived mainly in Finland, Paris, Munich, and Geneva. In his first narrative, *Land of His Own* (1906), Tuglas realistically yet poetically delineated a tenant farmer who craved for a farm of his own. The collections of short stories *You and I* (1908) and *The Evening Sky* (1913), reveal his attraction for neoromanticism flavored with nuances of symbolism and impressionism. This same tendency appears in his anthologies, *Destiny* (1917), *The Spirit of Oppression* (1920), and *The Resettlement of Souls* (1925). The Bohemian novel *Felix Ormusson* (1915) is the writer's most impressionistic work. It is the diary of a peculiar individualist, Ormusson, who rejects everything real. "Only that is beautiful which doesn't exist," he says, "Indulgence in fancies is better than any achievement." In the two-volume novel *Little Illimar* (1937–1938), Tuglas enthusiastically reconstructs the inner world of his childhood. The novel involves a multitude of strikingly clear characters, and it shows a definite inclination towards the poetic realism of his earlier work.

As a successor of Suits, he became a professor at Tartu University in 1944. Since then he has written very little in belles-lettres. His total contribution, however, now exceeds 130 titles. To these belong his travelogues, *The Journey to Spain* (1918), *The Journey to North-Africa* (3 vols., 1928–1930), *The First Trip Abroad* (1945), and his biographies, *Juhan Liiv* (1914), *Anton H. Tammsaare* (1919), *William Shakespeare* (1920), *Henrik Ibsen* (1920), and *Karl Rumor-Ast* (1930). Tuglas has composed a number of memoirs, such as *Early Years* (1940) and *Emigré Years* (1960), as well as numerous collections of essays: *Echo of the Time* (1919), *Criticism* (8 vols., 1919–1936), *Marginalia* (1921), *The Literary Diary* (1921), and *Estonian Literary Society* (1932). A translator and prominent literary critic, Tuglas has kept a literary diary since 1906. The following extracts are taken from the work *Thoughts and Moods* (1960):

A good book reveals the soul of its author not only to the reader, but also to the writer himself. No writer remains the same after finishing a book. In writing a book, a writer lives many lives. They include a happy voyage across the New Land under the new-born sun, as well as the gloom of prison and its despair. They include a series of recreations of oneself from thousands of fragmentary thoughts and feelings. In bestowing gifts upon others, the writer above all bestows them on himself.

—:—:—

I understand why the ordinary reader is so attracted by books whose covers say they are based on real events. I am sometimes disappointed that what I read is merely the fruit of the imagination.

But it is not entirely imagination, for a book helps to lay bare those characteristics of a man which tend to remain concealed. Heroic literature frequently hastens the emergence of a hero, while crime literature frequently hastens the emergence of the criminal. In a biography of such a hero or such a criminal, their literary prototypes should be named.

"Life copies literature," wittily observed Oscar Wilde. He insisted that fogs appeared in London only after Turner had painted them. It is at least true that after they had been painted by Turner, people learned to notice them. We frequently do not feel or know that which we have within us until someone brings it to our attention.

—:—:—

It should be realized that form is only the envelope of content. Outside the artistic synthesis neither the one nor the other has independent worth. But it is possible to achieve this synthesis only with the aid of a highly developed form.

Form must serve as the embodiment of the thoughts, the feelings and the inner world of man. All discussions about the writer's technique are meaningless if an account is not taken of that rhythm of life and that energy which have to be depicted with its aid. In its pure state the method of form is of use only to morons.

—:—:—

Again and again attacks are made upon literary works because they are "tendentious." But the assailants do not take the trouble to consider the meaning of this "tendentiousness." It is impossible to imagine that any substantial work should not reflect, at least indirectly, the existing social situation and that it should not throw light upon social relations. Man is constantly thinking and weighing, and his thoughts and appraisals have their own "tendentiousness." If this were not true, whole genres, both of the ode and works of a satirical character, would disappear completely.

—:—:—

The point is not that "tendentiousness" in itself is harmful to art, but that, alone, it does not make a work of art.

By "tendentiousness" we mean the mood, the outlook and the convictions which the author himself entirely shares. All contriving, all half-measures are things of the devil.

"Tendentiousness" of great artistic value is reflected in the flesh and blood of vital human images and it infects the reader, stirring his emotions. Mere rhetoric, abstract truths and philosophizing in art convince no one.

The more objective the form of narrative, the less opportunity the writer has to express his ideas directly, personally. The author of a realistic novel cannot speak or campaign or polemicize on his own behalf. Only the choice of theme, its logical development and ideological insight can, in the ultimate analysis, reflect the author's "tendentiousness."

(Steven Andrews)

The didactic element of Tuglas' essay concurs with the concept of Giovanni Boccaccio, who considered literature as an instrument for the entertainment of society. The English poet Herbert George Wells also shared this belief. He declined to write for the sake of art and declared that "Literature is not jewelry; it has other aims than perfection." Communist governments impose socialist realism to reinforce their policies by means of literature.

Ernst Enno (1875–1934) associated with the Young Estonia group, although he was not a member. The anthologies of his poetry *The New Poems* (1909), *The Grey Songs* (1910), *The Bright Night* (1920), and *The Lost Home* (1920) were ignored for a long period of time because they are abstract and difficult to comprehend. Enno's main theme is oriental philosophy, interpreted mostly in terms of pantheistic doctrine. Although Enno lapses into clichés and repetitions, his expression is very musical, as in "She Came" taken from *The Grey Songs*:

> She came, and looked at me kindly,
> But not a word would she say.
> She came, and looked at me kindly,
> And then she hastened away.
>
> I rose and followed the footprints
> She had left behind in her flight.
> I rose and followed her footprints,
> And came to the mansion of Night.

"Night, tell me," I said, "where my love is.
Perhaps you have word for me."
"Night, tell me," I said, "where my love is."
But the dark night could not see.

Night stood there and looked at me strangely;
She was bound with a heavy chain.
Night stood there and looked at me strangely,
And I went on my way again.

And always I sought for those footprints
Till I deemed that my quest was won.
And always I sought for those footprints,
And I reached the court of the Sun.

"Sun, tell me," I said, "where my love is.
Perhaps you have something to tell."
"Sun, tell me," I said, "where my love is."
But the sun seemed bound by a spell.

The sun, he looked at me gravely;
So grave are those who know.
The sun, he looked at me gravely,
Till I felt that I must go.

And I went, and sought unhoping
Where I had not sought before,
And I found that the feet I was trailing
Led up to my own soul's door.

(W. K. Matthews)

Villem Grünthal-Ridala (1885–1942), a lecturer of Estonian language and literature at Helsinki University, placed strong emphasis upon his language, which is well-mastered but complex, and contains archaisms and provincialisms. In his collections of poetry, *Villem Grünthal's Songs* (1908), *The Distant Shore* (1914), *In the Storm and Wind* (1927), and *The Starfish* (1935), he portrayed the Estonian land and waters, minutely recording the myriad changes of the seasonal cycles. He introduced a quantitative verse system into the *Kunstdichtung* of Estonia.

Besides being a politician and vice-consul in Brazil, Karl Rumor (b. 1886; now in the United States), wrote an anthology of erotic stories, *The Fires in an Autumn Night* (1919). In the short stories and plays that followed this volume, Rumor stressed the coherence between spiritual affinity and sex, employing cynicism and irony. His novel *The Crucifix* (1960) ridicules certain fanatic religious practices in South-America.

August Gailit (b. 1891; died in Sweden, 1960) was born into an Estonian-Latvian family and became a leading prose writer of the Siuru group. Already in his first collection of fantastic stories, *The Merry-go-round of Satan* (1917), Gailit shows his preference for exceptional and exaggerated characters. The same approach, with added ironic overtones, dominates his best novel, *Toomas Nipernaadi* (1928). Nipernaadi is an author who travels about the countryside incognito and is mistaken for a vagabond:

> It was evident that he had traveled for several days because he looked tired and dusty. He didn't hurry, walked only for fun along the roads and woods, and rested under a bush, in the shadow of a tree, or in some shed near a swamp, and was content. Often he avoided the highway traffic, crossed meadows and fields, went astray in the forest and roamed through thickets until he found a way or a path. At times, he stayed on the shore of a lake or at a cove of a river where, certain of his solitude, he sang, playing a zither, or conversed with himself in a loud voice. He showed a great interest in observing birds and insects, particularly butterflies on a spear of grass. Then he jumped up and continued his journey. Afflicted with restlessness, he continually moved from place to place, as if searching for something.
>
> Sometimes he turned back without any apparent reason. The barking of a strolling dog or the caw of a crow could spoil his mood entirely. As long as he had enough bread in his pockets, he avoided people and passed villages in a roundabout way. When somebody approached, he quickly stepped

into the woods and waited patiently behind a tree, until the road was clear again.

Once he stopped at a cottage, took off his hat, and began to sing. As soon as the sleepy face of a man appeared in the window, he interrupted the song, turned his back, and fled rapidly. On one occasion, he caught many snakes in a swamp and carried them into an empty shed. In the evening he brought a hat filled with glow-worms. He sat on the ground and meditated, scrutinizing the tiny·strange lights and listening to the hostile hissing of snakes. Thus he fell asleep among these creatures. In the morning he was disappointed to find that all his pets were gone.

(Aleksis Rubulis)

The novel is composed of a sequence of seven short stories. It found wide acceptance at home and abroad. Gailit's next novel, *The Land of Our Fathers* (1935), deals with the war of independence, while another novel, *The Rough Sea* (1938), portrays the unusual lives of fishermen on an island. In exile, August Gailit wrote the novels *The Flaming Heart* (1945) and *Across the Restless Sea* (1951). In the latter he describes the tragic flight of Estonian men and women who escaped the Red Army by crossing the Baltic Sea and the varied behavior of these people in the face of danger. In Sweden Gailit also wrote the trilogy of short stories, *Do You Recall, My Dear?* (3 vols., 1951, 1955, 1959).

The vivid characterization, tension, and humor of the novel *The Spring* (2 vols., 1912–1913) made Oskar Luts (1887–1954) popular throughout the country. Influenced by Knut Hamsun's style, in 1914 Luts published the novel *It Is Written,* in which he let an artist judge all people according to his own standards. At this time, Oskar Luts abandoned romanticism, and in *The Life of Andrew* (1923), *The Affliction of Olga* (1926), and *The Quiet Corner* (1934), he adhered to realism.

Henrik Visnapuu (b. 1890; died in Long Island, 1951) was also a member of the Siuru and studied in Tartu and in Berlin. His first anthologies of poetry, *Amores* (1917), *Farewell, Ene!* (1918), and *The Wild Violet* (1920), are dominated by cynical sensualism. A vivid portrayal of the effects of frivolity, *The Flintstone* (1925) is filled with melancholy, a sense of guilt, and death. The few patriotic motives found in the latter work increase in number and strength in Visnapuu's *Songs of the Land of Virgin Mary*[17] (1927). A certain optimism pervades *The Sun and the Brook* (1932) and *The Northern Lights* (1938). Contemporary themes stand out in *The Baltic Sea* (1948) and in *The Milky Way* (1950). Visnapuu experimented with rhyme at both the beginning and the end of a verse. He achieved considerable originality in form.

 ## Expressionism and Neorealism

The Young Estonia group was active for only a few years, and with the outbreak of World War I it ceased to exist. Instead, the Siuru[18] movement was founded in 1917, which revived Estonian literature in an egocentric aspect. The chief representative and president of this movement was the poet Marie Under (b. 1883; now residing in Stockholm). In her first book, *Sonnets* (1917), Marie Under surprised her audience with her genuine and esthetically well-executed portrayal of nature, which heralded the birth of a great talent; however, conservative readers were shocked by her frank display of eroticism. The same motifs dominate her collections *The Early Spring* (1918) and *The Blue Sail* (1918). Influenced by German expressionists, she wrote *The Bleeding Wound* (1920), *The Heritage* (1923), and *Voice from the Shadows* (1927). Amid glimpses of delight, one senses the ominous presence of dismal moods, as seen at the beginning of the poem "Evening," included in *The Heritage:*

> Night is near: gates are shut and doors are barred.
> Ancient grief cuts deep and hard.

---

[17] The Catholic Church has dedicated the Baltic States to the Virgin Mary.
[18] A mythological fire-bird.

Light withdraws its burning bridge.
Hands, like empty gauntlets, droop. Blackness
    yawns beyond the ridge.

(Ants Oras)

The ballads in *Eclipse of Happiness* (1929) conjure up legendary episodes; atheism and depression are present. Already
at this stage, Marie Under had attained a distinctive and vigorous style. Her trips to Paris (1926), Rome (1929), and Vienna
(1929), as well as the influence of her religious mother, transformed her outlook into a stronger, more optimistic perspective, and her next volume, *A Stone Off the Heart* (1935), contains
such poems as "The Harp of David," "Adam," "Jacob and
Leah," and "Mary Magdalene." The poetess announced that
man has his roots in God. Her despair had subsided considerably, as if she had been relieved of a burden. Of all Marie
Under's books, *With Sorrowful Mouth* (1942) held most
appeal for Estonians, for it expressed their feelings about the
tragic annexation of their country by the Nazis and the Soviets.
During the Soviet invasion in 1944, Marie Under entrusted her
fate to the Baltic Sea and escaped to Sweden in a tiny boat. She
had dedicated some of her best poems to the Baltic Sea, and it
responded. In spite of another stone on her heart, the gentle and
frail poet took courage and became a speaker for her nation:

We Wait

The splendour of our tree lies torn and scattered,
The shade of death hangs over all that mattered.

Dispersed and dispossessed, as restless rangers,
We drift but past ourselves—our selves are strangers.

Yet tense, in large-eyed hope, we gaze and wait.
Our cross is heavy but our backs are straight.

We know, whatever burdens wrench our shoulders:
Life owes us justice! and the knowledge smoulders.

A cry from soul to soul drowns scorn and spite:
Bring, day of grace, thy liberating light!

Restore what we have lost, retrieve, retrieve
Our name, our face, the land for which we grieve.

Come, sacred day of hope, whose lightning flashes!
Thy children wait for thee in tears and ashes.

We wait. We keep our faith. We stand unbowed.
Thus life grows easier—thus death is proud.

(Ants Oras)

Marie Under wrote this poem on January 31, 1947, but published it in the volume *Sparks in Ashes* in 1954. It is marked with anguish and with an unyielding determination. Every sonorous verse is executed with virtuosity. To Professor Ants Oras, she is a poet "of striking symbolic depth and power."[19] Indeed, her style is varied; occasionally it is "meeker than a dove"; then, unexpectedly it shifts to a forceful mode and resounds with a prophetic and resentful accord, as in the "Indictment" from *Sparks in Ashes:*

I

I cry with all my people's lungs and lips:
A terrible, unbearable disease
Has struck our land—a blight of gallows-trees,
A plague of deadly fear that sears and grips.

Who comes to help? Now, instantly! The frail
And failing body cannot last: make speed!
But weakly rings my voice, a birdlike wail
That dies: the heedless world is cold indeed.

The old men's agony, the children's sobs,
The sounds of anguish, stifled in the night,
The silence of despair, the wound that throbs
Are only idle tales for men of might.

The world is blind, the world is deaf, we cry
Unheard, for power is callous or insane:
But those have pity who are numbed with pain,
But those have hearts who suffer—you and I.

---

[19] See Ants Oras' *Estonian Poetry* (New York, 1957), p. 10.

II

The bilious sky's distorted shadows loom,
My whirling thoughts claw at the storm and wage
Their war like beasts, grown desperate in their cage,
My torment sinks its teeth into our gloom.

I must stir up the ashes—but for whom?
To rouse and quicken our insensate age.
I must stir up the spark of generous rage.
Drum of my soul's despair, denounce and doom!

Now night is near, and all my sorrow spills
Into the dusk. The darkness staggers, whipped
By harsh, condemning cries—a storming surge.

Relentless, flaming indignation fills
My sleepless eyes: my eyes accuse and urge,
And only God can bear their burning script.

III

I come from very far and and very late,
Bare semblance of myself, pursued and bowed
By faithful wintry thoughts of home that shroud
The sights of spring: yet spring unbars its gate.

The way is open, but deep grudges grate
Upon my darkened mind that notes the loud
Delight of May, the apple trees that crowd
The flowering orchards: notes them, black with hate.

Thee, Guardian Angel, claims my scornful call,
I cry for balm, with venom in my chalice,
And yet I could be meeker than a dove.

I see and feel—but what? The pull and shove
Of cunning fiends? The downward drag of malice?
Is sweetness of revenge the crown of all?

(Ants Oras)

Widely diverse phenomena of life are encompassed within
the scope of Marie Under's contemplative and transcendental

cognition. In "Ecstasy" (1917) the poet eagerly accepts the blossoms of life and admits that her "every nerve vibrates to rapt delight." However, she also acknowledges death, for it "grants her something that life had not given her: the ability to sustain a total, ultimate experience."[20]

The International PEN, the Finnish Writers Union, and the Bavarian Academy of Arts and Sciences elected Marie Under an honorary member. Her last book, *On the Brink* (1963), is filled with reservation:

On the Brink

Times rushed. Times whirled and whirred.
Their breath stays, rank and eery.
A second time, a third.
Brief lies of soothing years.
Time to untime all times. . . .

What was the last bird's query?
I've rhymed my answering rhymes.
Blind silence stares and sneers.

(Ants Oras)

Anton Hansen Tammsaare (1878–1940) collaborated closely with the Young Estonia circle. At the beginning of his career, Tammsaare wrote poetry, as well as about thirty naturalistic rural stories. Some of his stories are highly critical of society, as, for example, "Number 17":

"Number 17!"
"What, sir? I am here!" an elderly woman replied in a weak but eager voice.
"You didn't deliver the newspaper to Mr. T. on N. street yesterday. Do you have an explanation?"
"I haven't delivered? I did."
"He hasn't received it. Came here today to complain."
Number 17 doesn't have any answer. She understands that

---

[20] See Aleksis Rannit's "Tribute to Marie Under at Eighty" in *Books Abroad*, Spring 1963, pp. 125–130.

the young gentleman didn't make any error and he wouldn't complain without a reason.

"Do it today. And don't forget it!"

"Sure, why shouldn't I deliver it. He lives in a four-story stone building. His apartment is in the garret. It is a hell of a job to climb those stairs."

Number 17 wants to talk to somebody, to disclose the burden of her work. But she is told to keep silent, for her conversation disturbs others at work. Besides, it has been clear for ages what she wants to expound. For many years Number 17 has delivered newspapers. Quite a few times she attempted to reveal her misfortune and every time she failed, for she was warned to maintain peace. Her complaints would bother the employees. At first it never occurred to her why such explanation could be a nuisance. She didn't accuse a single soul and had no intention of facilitating her labor. No, she would never want that. She understands: submit to the will of God and the problem will resolve itself, perhaps even tomorrow. In the meantime she will bear her cross patiently, as long as it is in compliance with God's commandments. But it would be nice to share trouble with people and to feel relieved.

At every peremptory shout Number 17 would start, shrink into a corner, and become absorbed in thought. Thus she did not bother people while in the office, nor on the streets dragging newspaper stacks, nor toiling home tired in the evening. And what should she contemplate? There had been no change within a number of years: she arrived at the dispatch office, received the usual number of newspapers, distributed them, and returned home. In the morning, the bag was rather heavy, it bent her double. She entered humid and stuffy basements and waited until residents answered the doorbell. Often it was a luxurious apartment; at times she had to reach the garret. In winter it was always cold; in summer, sultry. She walked and carried, until her head began to spin. Finally, her legs refused to obey. It was hardly possible to resist the temptation of leaning on the railing for a moment. However, she had to move, for her master shouted:

"Number 17!"

"Yes, sir! I am here."

"Yesterday you didn't deliver the newspaper to Mr. X."

Number 17 has begun to forget her name. In all these years she hasn't heard it once. Should there be any complaint, superiors would ask:

"Where do you live?"

"On S. street."

"Oh! Number 17 is in charge of it. Well, I shall tell her."

And so on: constantly Number 17 and Number 17. Even at home, where her son lived with his wife and children, she was called "old woman."

Today she could scarcely overcome weariness. A gusty autumn rain splashed against her face. All streets were covered with slush, and smaller alleys were not illuminated. Only in the distance a lantern shimmered, reflecting its dim light in a muddy puddle. Number 17 proceeded gropingly, but still delivered to the readers information about crimes and misfortune, articles on politics, science, literature, and the arts. The content didn't influence Number 17. All she thought about was supplying subscribers with this news as quickly as possible.

Upon her return home, Number 17 fell into her bed without supper. The morning came, but she did not rise. The daughter-in-law asked:

"What is the matter with you? Don't you want to get up?"

"I don't have the strength. All my bones ache, I am sick at heart."

"Oh, have you collapsed suddenly? You were always able to work!"

"Sometimes we just can't," she replied. Then she called her grandson and sent him to the office to inform her superiors that Number 17 could not work.

"Our grandmother will not deliver your newspapers," the boy notified them. "She lies ill in bed."

"What? Sick?"

"Yes."

"What is her number?"

"Seventeen."

Two weeks passed.

"Number 17!" a voice resounded in the office.

No response. The young executive called once more with the same result.

"Liisa, can't you hear? He is calling you," said one of the women. "Weeks have passed, but you still don't know your number."

A young red-cheeked girl stepped forward.

"You are replacing Number 17. I haven't heard a word about her for a long time," the executive told the girl. "Do you want to work here?"

"Oh, yes!" the girl replied happily, for she needed a job.

"Well, we have Number 17 again. However, I must remind you that yesterday you neglected to deliver the newspaper to Mr. N. on S. street. He was here to complain."

The girl became confused and embarrassed, but couldn't say a word.

"Try to serve as honestly as did the former Number 17," advised the gentleman, while the girl blushed more than ever.

"True, the old woman will not come," one of the employees mentioned. "The dead don't deliver newspapers."

"Is she dead?" the executive asked.

"Yesterday a church service was—"

"Where?"

"At St. John's."

"I was there; however, I didn't notice it."

An ironic smile appeared on the face of the employee as she said:

"You didn't know her name, sir. Therefore, you couldn't —"

"Of course," he admitted. "According to my list she was Number 17."

"Very true, sir. She always wanted to confess her sorrows to you. Apparently—" her voice ceased, for she was admonished:

"Tsssh—You are disturbing us."

The woman grew calm, just as Number 17 had so often done, for people avoid listening to sad stories.

(Aleksis Rubulis)

Tammsaare's first novel, *The Farmer of Kõrboja* (1922), is closer to impressionism. It describes a conflict between two social classes. Poor Katku Villu feels unfit for wealthy Anna and commits suicide. The stupendous five-volume novel *The Truth and Justice* (1926–1933) is dedicated to the peasantry. To Tammsaare, man is both master and servant of the earth. The earth remains just; it rewards when man is true, as when he works in the sweat of his brow. Structurally, it is somewhat vague, but the description is explicit and most of the nearly two hundred characters involved bear distinctive traits. Once Tammsaare said that every work should bear characteristics of its author; however, it must be presented to a reader in an intelligible manner. His later novel *The Life and the Love* (1934) speaks of romantic impulses, but the allegory *Old Nick of Hell Valley* (1939) is based on folklore.

Hugo Raudsepp (1883–1951) was the greatest Estonian playwright. Some of his more significant comedies are *The Demobilized Father* (1923), *Sinimandria* (1927), *Mikumärdi* (1929), which became especially popular, and *The Idler* (1935). Most characters are presented in a grotesque aspect; the language is witty and cynical. Among his later works are short stories and the plays *The Flags in a Storm* (1937) and *The Man with Trumps in His Hand* (1938). After World War II Raudsepp was forced to create comedies favorable to the occupation; however, his life ended in a Soviet prison.

Artur Adson (b. 1889; now living in Stockholm) began with juvenile love poetry in the collections *The Burning Soul* (1917) and *The Old Lantern* (1919). *The Garland of Roses* (1920) and *Transit* (1927), however, contain a notable variety of themes, ·with emphasis on social problems presented in an invigorated classical form. Adson is also the author of many plays. Of his historical dramas, the most thrilling is *Four Kings* (1931), based on the Estonian uprising of 1343. In *The Father of Songs and the Poetess* (1930), he depicted the relationship between F. R. Kreutzwald and Lydia Koidula. While in exile he has written several books of memoirs, among them *The Book of the Siuru* (1949) and *The Book About Theater* (1958). Adson is the second husband of Marie Under.

Under the National Flag

With the declaration of independence in 1918, all facets of cultural life began to boom. The press became free; many literary journals were founded. The number of newspapers and periodicals exceeded 300. Of every 1,000 inhabitants, three were university students. About 200 Estonians annually pursued their studies abroad. In 1920, the theater resumed its performances under improved conditions. Many provincial playhouses opened. In painting, French post-impressionism was introduced by K. Mägi (1878–1925) and V. Ormisson (1892–1940), Italian futurism by A. Vabbe (1892–1961), and contemporary German tendencies by portraitist P. Raud (1865–1930) and his brother K. Raud (1865–1943), who gradually developed highly original techniques. The Pallas School of Arts in Tartu played an important role under the leadership of professors N. Triik (1884–1940) and A. Vabbe. Sculptor A. Adamson (1855–1929) excelled in wood carving. After studying Egyptian art, J. Koort (1883–1935) applied various forms to his modern works. E. Wiiralt (1898–1954), Estonia's foremost engraver, achieved international recognition. Vocal music was revived under the modern composers J. Aavik (b. 1884; now living in Sweden), C. Kreek (1889–1962), A. Vedro (1890–1945), and Enn Võrk (1905–1962).

The critic and professor of comparative literature Gustav Suits accentuated the nature and evolution of West-European literature. Estonian students were more proficient in German than in Russian; they preferred Shakespeare, Dante, Byron, Goethe, and Schiller to Pushkin and Tolstoy, since for centuries they had been bound to the West by political, cultural, and religious affinities.

The contribution of Ants Oras (b. 1900; now residing in Gainesville, Fla.) has not been adequately estimated, although Estonian intellectuals have issued a scholarly book in his honor. In this volume, *Estonian Poetry and Language* (1965), Professor Aleksis Rannit says that Oras has "built an arch of human truth and artistic measure." When, in the 1920's, the circle *Logomancers* emerged to counteract the members of the Siuru and of Young Estonia, its pseudoliterary presentation of political ideology threatened to turn poetry into journalism. Oras, having studied languages, literature, and philosophy at the universities of Tartu, Leipzig, and Oxford, laid the foundations of humanism and artistic expression for the whole literary trend with his exhaustive critical analyses. As early as 1919, he insisted on firmly disciplined expressive form and impeded the tendency towards flabbily formed *laissez-faire, laissez-passer.* Ants Oras promulgated a poetry which illustrates central human experiences rather than passing fads and mere play and thus strengthened a trend already represented by Marie Under and Gustav Suits.

In 1933, Ants Oras became a professor of English at the University of Tartu; at present he is a professor and chairman of the English Department at the University of Florida. Paralleling his instructional activities, Professor Oras has produced numerous books of literary criticism, a few of which are: *The Critical Ideas of T. S. Eliot* (1932), *Notes on Some Miltonic Usages, Their Background and Later Development* (1938), *On Some Aspects of Shelley's Poetic Imagery* (1938), *Pause Patterns in Elizabethan and Jacobean Drama: an Experiment in Prosody* (1960), *Marie Under* (1963), and the volume of essays *Towards Broader Horizons* (1961). The latter best reveals the character of his great intellect. Ants Oras favors strength, clear outlines, and the exposition of definite ideas with the force of conviction; he stands for spaciousness rather than the narrowness which induces claustrophobia. Asked about literary movements, Professor Oras replied: "I don't care about isms. For me only the individual work counts, no matter what its ism. The ism I hate is chaoticism." Oras has published several hundred essays and articles in the press and scholarly journals and has strengthened Western traditions in Estonia by translating Goethe's *Faust* into Estonian, as well as the works of Poe,

Shakespeare, Molière, Shaw, Pope, Stevenson, Baudelaire, Vergil, Keats, Zielinski, and Thackerey. He has also translated many Estonian works into English and German. According to Professor Alo Raun, his *Umdichtung* is full of music and color; it is "a masterly example of living poetry."

In this period of cultural growth the former school principal and member of Parliament, August Mälk (b. 1900; since 1944 in Stockholm) created his novels *The Stoney Nest* (1932), *The Flowering Sea* (1935), *Under the Face of the Sky* (1937), and *The Good Harbor* (1942), all of which depict the lives of seasiders and islanders in a manner similar to that of Hamsun and Tuglas. *The Dead Homes* (1934) and *Masters of the Baltic Sea* (1936) are historical novels. In the former he treats of the Great Northern War with realistic features. Mälk is also the author of a number of plays and short stories. The intricacies of family life are skillfully handled in his novel *The Vernal Soil* (1963).

Heiti Talvik (b. 1904; died in Siberia, 1945) struggled with despondency and a sense of predestined catastrophe. "A deer has drowned in the swamp of my bosom," he wrote in the poem "The Swamp." In the volumes *The Fever* (1934) and *Doomsday* (1937), he anticipated false prophets and the destruction of the world. Noted for his wit and his literal use of epigrams, Talvik was a poet-prophet and a Baudelairean kind of existentialist.

Talvik's wife, Betti Alver (b. 1906; now living in Estonia) made her debut with prose, then published two novels. Influenced by Ants Oras, in the collections of poetry *Dust and Fire* (1936) and *The Tree of Life* (1942) she clung to J. S. Mill's doctrine of the plurality of causes. She is constantly searching for the good within the framework of neosymbolist and neoclassicist esthetics. Betti Alver's temper is restrained; now and then her impressionistic stanzas manifest unresisting acquiescence, as in "Snow in May":

> Buds face the dawn with a mirroring glimmer,
> Endlessly wistful, endlessly distant;
> Some open, a glow

Reddens within them, like torches, but dimmer—
Shyly subdued, as they meet, unresistant,
The snow.

(Ants Oras)

The collection of selected poetry *The Starry Hour* (1966)
reveals her refined style as well as her abandonment of cosmopolitanism.

In *Sonnets* (1935), *The Old Homes* (1937), and *The Corn-
Drying Kiln* (1939), Bernard Kangro (b. 1910; now in Sweden)
immortalized kaleidoscopic scenes of Estonian fauna and flora,
for example, "Forest" from *The Old Homes:*

Every winter the hare would come to our garth
To repair the season's losses,
And squirrels would scuttle on log and thatch,
And the goat champ the wall's gray mosses.

A troop of partridge would rise in flight
From the barn with a sound of snapping;
The banded magpie would drop at our door,
And the woodpecker keep on tapping.

As tame as a kitten and eager for milk,
A hedgehog slipped in from the tillage;
And one black and sinister autumn night
The wolf came to slaughter and pillage.

The covetous aspen had reached our gate,
And lindens the garden fences;
Red ants crawled in thousands all over the walls;
And the death-tick pierced our defences.

The death-tick kept ticking the doom of our croft
Till at length its days were counted:
The rustling forest invaded our garth,
And leaves sprang where smoke had mounted.

(W. K. Matthews)

His postwar volumes *The Burnt Tree* (1945), *The Seventh
Night* (1947), and *The Hearth* (1949) are more inward in

character and, at times, mystic. Memories of his captive home intermingle with supernatural phenomena. In *The Hearth* Kangro adhered to the Shakespearean sonnet; however, he also practiced free verse, as in "Sorrowful Lion":

On my font, which is hewn from a gray and massive
Block of rough granite,
Is a trammelled lion enclosed between symbols.

Year after year in the North's frozen forests
I roam, and my vision is keen,
And my footsteps are bold.

But there in the dusk of the walls and imprisoned
In stone is the lion,
And above him a dry tree's tangle of branches.

He has long been a captive of
Frigid granite.
Blinding tears strengthlessly
Course down over his heavy
Pads, now grown palsied
From far expeditions to the South's giant sunlands.

(W. K. Matthews)

In recent years Kangro has published five novels, among them *Tartu* (1962), which deals with the intellectual elite and graphically depicts student life in the university city where the author studied and later served on the faculty.

Karl Ristikivi (b. 1912; now in Sweden) continued the realistic tradition of Vilde and Tammsaare in his novels *Fire and Iron* (1938), *In a Strange House* (1940), and *The Garden* (1942). In these works he exposed the nature of various social strata and their interactions. Ristikivi's exile served as a type of metamorphosis. His fantastic narrative *All Souls' Night* (1953) reads like a mixture of the hallucinations in Herman Hesse's novel *Der Steppenwolf* and *Alice in Wonderland*. His novels *The Burning Banner* (1961), *The Last City* (1962), and *Riders of Death* (1963) deal with European history. The historical

novel *The Song of Joy* (1966) is more optimistic and expresses
a deep religious sentiment.

Unlike Marie Under, who excels in treating both spiritual
and physical dimensions, Aleksis Rannit (b. 1914; now living
in New Haven, Conn.) has distinguished himself by investing
his works with intellectual power. Actually, each of these great
poets serves as a complement to the other. They do have common motifs; one of them is the sea. The treatment, however,
is different. To Marie Under, the sea is more divine, mystic,
and tenebrous. In the poem "Look, the Sea Rises" (1930), she
envisions the sea as satanic, a dangerous phenomenon, in an
approach similar to that of Theodor Storm. Rannit, on the other
hand, does not worship the sea. The poet's analysis of the universe is merely a presentation of his esthetics; it expresses his profound admiration of "hard-and-fluid harmony" and of "static
dynamics," e.g., "The Sea," taken from *The Dry Radiance:*

Once again I am before you, Great Ancestor Sea,
I surrender to you my frail body, my bare feet.

Mute, with thirst of fish ashore, I sigh with gaping mouth;
know: you are my sole sensation, my sole urge, impulse.

Light playing in silent white, your waving spiral rings,
thrusting me and touching my space, holds me like a frame,

holds me . . . then with jarring motion, spins me with all
    strength—
this is my life out of life-death, my living ascent.

Ascension into the depth, and then the most triumphant
    flight
is to your delicate surface touch, my tepid Love.

Bursting open, open, far off, the huge globeflower moon
spreads out over you her silvery-yellowish gown,

sheerly, quiet. Night and silence. Your clear song of joy
vaults up sharply like the timeless brilliance of the sky.

Just where is this instrument from? What clockwork keeps
     time
to this finely shaded, tuned, this precision-cut tide?

Every measured tremor, every trembling bit of surf
follows cosmic order, strictly attuned to the world.

Listen: listening to your planet's pulse, there brightly bend
whispering sand, dance-falling bird, feather-whirling wind.

I know: before mutiny arose in formless forms,
way even before the Word spoke, Rhythm ruled them firm.

Through your floodwashed boulder range the light of
     Rhythm strikes
as does through the hardest of stones, the dark diorite.

Hard and fluid! final beauty, form as flexible
as architectonic music, growing like crystal—

as perfection moved and finished, as that surging skill,
you're the clear and distinct sea, your own perennial school.

. . . Will you then take, free this craving glance, this yearn-
     ing face,
Rhythm, perfected in stream—Rhythm, my giant fate?

(Emery E. George)

Both a connoisseur and a theoretician of art, Aleksis Rannit
strives for perfection. The poet admits that he is form-
possessed. Poetry or any creative art, to him, should embody the
analytic of the sublime and, therefore, exclude emotionalism.
In *The Dry Radiance* Rannit ascertains that true art neither
weeps nor cries. He addresses Byron as the "poet of thunder"
and divulges that he prefers the "slow flame of syllables" to
their lightning. Aleksis Rannit has dedicated a number of
poems to the engraved line.

Line

Love toward graven line,
toward thou, all illuminating power!
thou, all ennobling rune—
Line of the thunderbolt and not the thunder!

All binding and all bounding line,
accurate as the rhyme of death—
Pheidias,[21] Ingres,[22] Wiiralt,[23]
Bach, and Paul Valéry.

I have broken faith with colour.
Now my verses measure for the line—
for thee, line perfection engendered
in the ascetic square of the mind.

(Henry Lyman)

In his works Rannit searches for the transcendental balance of Eros and Thanatos, for "the music of the intellect" and "the mathematics of the soul." "All will turn into earth," the poet writes, "only the soul of form will survive." Constantly seeking new ontological expressions for his own works, Rannit shows his respect for the "objective subjectivity" of others:

At the Picasso Exhibition

> "[Picasso's] distorted human faces are perhaps our true likeness, when we are seen by the angels"—Jacques Maritain, *Creative Intuition in Art and Poetry*.

Our gluttonous spirits shake with hunger,
In our throats the gum has gotten stuck—
for here everyone has had to let go,
and even those scream who were born dumb.

But the public—dead fleshheaps—take it in.
Mutely they stare (faces of putrid fish) ;
smirk: kindles to irreverence of laymen,
to roaring laughter: "Get a load of this!"

And as moths' wings, so are our weightless accents.
Banal beauty turns to old heroin.
This is how they made fun of wholesome Rembrandt.
It's how they laughed at fiery Van Gogh.

---

[21] A Greek sculptor who lived in the fifth century B.C.
[22] A French historical painter (1780–1867).
[23] An Estonian engraver (1898–1954).

It has lasted long now—that same laughter
in the fateful and satanic ring.
Here, it's the Lord's knife dissecting the Zeitgeist,
there—it's the hostile pedestrian.

No one gets singled out. Man's face is told
in this art: the torn heart of the times,
the formula for ironic thought,
the tribune of archaic modern tone.

Semblance holds paradox: is then the artist
master or a witch's brood, a clown
in the ring? Do all others despise
his music, which whiplashes our planet,

Which as with straw will frolic with our minds,
then fling its shadow on the flame as lightly?
Dark method, O brush stroke burning blind—
amidst boredom we hear your lemur's laughter!

(Emery E. George)

Aleksis Rannit dedicated the following poem to Boris Vilde
(1908–1942), Estonian poet, essayist, ethnologist, and linguist
who wrote mostly in French and was executed by the Nazis in
Paris in 1942. Vilde was the founder of the periodical *Résistance,* which gave the French underground movement its
name.

Boris Vilde

"What I like in music is the introduction to
death"—Boris Vilde, from the *Prison Diary.*

As quiet shot, drunk with light, resounding,
reached to your evening—that was not death.
It was the only music, yes, resounding:
tender as minds dawning or light-drunk death,
quiet as shot, drunk with light, resounding.

A parting thought of love awoke as echo
when from the shot there sprang a flowering rose.

Fallen, you are yet transfigured as echo—
your name, bright as the flower we call a rose.
A parting thought of love awoke as echo.

Your luminous mind is like the clear morning
near summer seas at your Virumaa.[24]
Now they are with you: your new life's morning,
and night, in which you dreamed your Virumaa.
Your luminous mind is like the clear morning,

quiet as shot, resounding, drunk with light.

(Emery E. George)

Rannit studied literature, philosophy, esthetics, and art at several European universities as well as at Columbia. He was a professor of the history of art in Germany from 1946 until 1952, and since 1961 has been a professor and curator of Russian and East European Collections at Yale University. In 1962 he was elected a member of the International Academy of Arts and Letters in Paris. His collections of poems include: *In the Frame of a Window* (1937), *The Shake of the Hand* (1945), *The Enclosed Distance* (1956), *The Dry Radiance* (1963), *The Sea* (1964), *22 Poems* (1965), and *Kaljud* (1969). He is also well known for his essays and criticism.

Venetian Venus

The dalliance of late summer's fruits
on the open caravel of fancies,
strolls
on the cloudless piazetta of smiles,
celestial night-gathered strength
in the humming Giorgione morning—
Angels remote from your own home lagoons.
The thinning hair of our evenings,
the tardy waves of our happiness,
the deadly silence of our fulfillment—

---

[24] A northeastern district of Estonia.

Suddenly,
much
sand of despair.
The dead sea of oblivion.
The sea,
and above it,
against the splintering wall of the night—
the yellow elbows of lightning.

(Ruth Speirs)

In 1959, while on a Ford Foundation grant for his creative artistry, he visited the Mediterranean and Greece. On the Island of Cyprus an archer impressed Rannit with his expert demonstration of sharpshooting. For Rannit "the tension between the bow and the arrow was an esthetic sensation *per se*," and it inspired the poem "Cyprus," which expresses the poet's esthetic conviction. In several of his essays Rannit asserted that the form of any artistic creation must always be stronger than the content.

Cyprus

Again this winter in the skies,
this cunning artist bowman,
these Cyprian rocks,
these russet crystals blaze
that essence
          partakes of form.

(Henry Lyman)

In contrast with Avalon, an island paradise in Celtic legend, Rannit portrayed Lendonakía as a site of frustration which he visualized in his dream:

Lendonakía[25]

So faithfully recalled,
Lendonakía,
unforgettable headland,
never visited by me.

[25] A fictitious, fantastic panorama in Greece.

Oblong trunks of mountains under sea.
Shavings of moonlight,
    wavering in river pools.
Lanterns running bridges
    arching over the Karánis.[26]
Dead windows of the bungalows.
Dead leaves ringing in the heat.
Treestumps and their great dead eyes.
The bastard of my shadow, multifaced.

    Lendonakía—
blister on the memory.

                (Henry Lyman)

"Skyritis," in which Rannit's typical symbolism is exemplified
by vast seas and in towering mountains, continues to project
him into the philosophy of cosmism and conjures up the perpetual rhythm of the universe. The white foamy billows sig-
nify his friends, just warriors with their unstained banners
fallen for Estonia's freedom:

             Skyritis[27]

Even from here,
the Skyritian heights,
I can see thee,
    waves,—
waves like glasses raised by friends,
steaming like livid steeds,
waves like banners of the fallen.

                (Henry Lyman)

Already in his first volumes of short stories, *Under the Gate*
(1936) and *The Barren Tree* (1940), Valev Uibopuu (b. 1913;
now in Sweden) skillfully analyzed the inner nature of man.
His novel *Nobody Hears Us* (1948) depicts the Soviet invasion
of Estonia and is carried out in esthetic distance. It became a

[26] A river.
[27] A mountain range in Greece.

best seller among the refugees of many nations. Uibopuu's latest stories are collected in *Alas for By-gone Days* (1949), *The Everlasting Village* (1954), and *Mosaic* (1962).

Arvo Mägi (b. 1913; now in Stockholm) has written numerous essays and reviews. His *roman à clef, Silver Youth* (1949), is based upon the varying milieux of the university city of Tartu. Mägi gained fame with the novels *Circles in the Water* (1952), *The Deluge* (1954), and *The Gates of Paradise* (1960), which display his keenness of judgment. Social and religious conflicts form the subject of his medieval novel *Dance into the Twilight* (1964).

World War II is relived in the collection of short stories *Only a Man* (1949) by Ilmar Talve (b. 1919; now a professor at the University of Turku), who served in the Finnish military forces. Contrary to the traditional Baltic propensity to portray heroes, Talve's characters possess all human weaknesses. On the other hand, bold characters and strict technique prevail in the refugee novel *The Snowed-in House* (1952). *Juhanson's Travels* (1959) is the humorous narrative of a former warrior. Professor Talve is also the author of a number of scholarly works.

Latvian Literature

Folklore

There is reason to believe that folk songs, the treasure of Latvian literature, are almost as old as the language itself. The vestiges of some stanzas can be traced back to the Age of Athens and the great migration of people. However, the first preserved authentic evidence was written in 1170 by Saxo Grammaticus concerning Kurish warriors, a tribe of western Latvia who landed on the island Öland, occupied Yarnlok harbor, and while awaiting another Danish attack, danced and sang their heroic songs.

The metrics and the style of the folk songs developed fully during the seventh and eighth centuries, but the songs really flourished from the thirteenth to the sixteenth centuries. These folk songs helped to mould the Latvian mentality and still play a significant role among Latvian writers, composers, and the people in general. The number of songs is immense and they encompass all occasions from cradle to grave:

> I was born singing, I grew up singing,
> I passed through life singing;
> And, singing, my soul ascended
> Into the garden of the Son of God.

In 1764, Johann G. Herder moved to Latvia, and during five active years he studied folklore and encouraged its collection. In his books *Volkslieder* (1779) and *Stimmen der Völker in Liedern* (1806), he published eleven Latvian songs in German translation. Several other clergymen expressed their interest in the ancient songs, particularly Gustavus von Bergmann in the *Erste Sammlung Lettischer Sinngedichte* (1807) and *Zweyte Sammlung Lettischer Sinn-oder Stegreifs Gedichte* (1808) as well as the country clergyman Daniel Wahr in his *Palzmareeschu Dseesmu Krahjums* (1807), upon which Sir Walter Scott based his article "Lettish Popular Poetry" in *The Foreign Quarterly Review* (Vol. VIII, no. 15 [1831]). Krišjānis Barons (1835–1923) devoted his entire life to collecting folk songs.

Thus, the Archives of Latvian Folklore has registered over one million folk songs with 13,093 melodies, 300,905 fairy tales, 53,745 legends, 450,313 riddles, 334,196 folk beliefs, 244,432 sayings and proverbs, 48,442 charms, 9,520 folk dances, and 28,986 anecdotes. The verb "to sing" has over fifty synonyms in Latvian.

In the songs a significant place is given to the raising of children. With great wisdom these songs teach parents how to take care of their children and educate them to be honest, diligent, obedient, and responsible. The ancient Latvians esteemed these virtues very highly:

> Let him work, whoever works,
> Let him work singing;
> Let him sleep, whoever sleeps,
> Let him sleep crying.

Lazy, drunk, and wicked people were not respected. Mental qualities were always considered superior to material wealth. When a girl was courted by several suitors and her mother was puzzled in choosing the proper son-in-law, the daughter contended:

> Value, mother, thoughts of men,
> Not their rye in granaries;
> Some man's wisdom is worth more
> Than the richest corn bins.

The folk songs also reveal traditions. We discover that in family life great honor and obedience were shown to the parents. Father had the decisive word. Mother, however, was more treasured and revered. Latvian folklore discloses various mythological mothers. The Roman historian Tacitus mentions that the ancient Balts worshipped *Matrem Deum*. If a father died, his oldest son became the head of a family. The folk literature pays special heed to the orphan, who was always delineated as a virtuous person, respected by all.

Young sons and young daughters,
Obey your own parents;
The sun is in the sky forever,
Not even for life your father and mother.

There were two, there were two
Who could hardly sleep:
The one was a honey bee,
The other was my mother.

I lit a splint, then a candle,
But my room was still dark;
As soon as my mother entered,
All illuminated at once.

Oh my dear brother,
Let's live friendly as two doves.
You wish me well, I wish you well,
That will be worth living.
What do we both gain
By doing or wishing evil?

A great number of songs speak of young people in love, of courtship and engagement. A wedding, combined with a send-off and reception, was celebrated for several days by continuous singing and dancing. The food and beverage supply was always sufficient. Such feasts started with a common singing of love by the bride and bridegroom as well as close relatives, particularly the mother-in-law, until it turned into a song of war. Another similar tradition that is still observed is the Līgo Festival on St. John's eve, on the 23rd of June. Etymologically, *līgo* means "rejoicing" or "singing." It is the refrain of innumerable songs. Superstitious tradition requires that all people wear wreaths of oak leaves or flowers. The homes, gates, and even the cattle are decorated in order to procure God's blessing and protection from evil. People walk through the fields from one farmstead to another, then gather around the bonfire, eat, drink, dance and sing. These songs are witty, full of teasing humor, but there is no trace of personal insult. Young girls and even elderly women joke with the boys and men, and vice versa:

> Shake and tremble, aspen leaf,
> While the wind is blowing;
> Thus our boys are trembling,
> While talking to girls.

> Proud fellows walked a road
> And carried all their wealth:
> They had rye, they had barley,
> All in one pocket.

> Let be busy, whoever is busy,
> A honey bee, she is busy;
> Let be lazy, whoever is lazy,
> Our neighbor's daughter, she is lazy.

> Young boys prayed to God
> In church every Sunday:
> Our Father, Hail Mary,
> Grant me a pretty girl.

When the time comes to part, all the guests express in song that they didn't mean any evil; they were singing only for the sake of entertainment and humor, and they thank the hosts for their hospitality:

> Bless, oh God, the place
> Where we ate, where we drank;
> May here grow two rye-ears
> At the end of each stalk.

These songs are so extensive and true that scholars can base their history textbooks on them. They don't brag of conquering foreign countries or speak of vengeance. The sole obligation is to protect their own people and terrain. Relatives formed military units, which were called *karogs* ("banners"). The warriors were dressed in brown uniforms, wore sable hats, and

carried swords. The songs disclose that the ancient Latvians had
to provide their own armaments:

> My mother wove me a belt,
> My father forged a sword,
> While my youngest sister
> Embroidered me a banner.

When the command was given to move, the warrior mounted
his horse and said, "I must go to the place where swords divide
the land." He departed, leaving behind "rye and barley sown
but not harvested," his "steed raised but not broken in," and his
"true love courted but not married."

> I'd rather die in a war
> Than at the roadside;
> Great men fall in a war,
> But dogs at the roadside.

> I laid down my own head
> Defending my fatherland's borders.
> I'd rather lose my young life
> Than my fatherland's freedom.

Women were the chief singers and connoisseurs for they
were the hearts of families, while men had to struggle with
nature and their external enemies. Nevertheless, there are many
exclusively masculine songs, regarding war, hunting, beekeep-
ing, and so forth. It was also a custom to select a dozen strong
men and to have them sit at an oak table. Each of the men
subsequently sang a song and emptied an oaken beer mug. The
procedure continued until each of the twelve men sang twelve
songs. All of the 144 songs with different words and melody had
to be about oaks. In Latvian folk literature men are often
compared to oaks.

Both Latvian and foreign scholars have conducted considerable research on the style and metrics of the folk songs; however,
the field is far from exhausted. The dactyl is preserved only in

ancient rituals and other religious customs. The great majority of the songs have been made up of trochaic dipodies, divided by caesuras. Rhythm varies slightly due to the omission of unstressed syllables. If a double-foot has to be expanded, usually the vowel *i* is inserted; rarely is it replaced with *a, e,* or *u.* Although strict common metric rules dominate, the folk songs vary in style. Rhythmic and grammatical accents sometimes contradict each other.

The language is rich in alliteration. Anaphoras and refrains are rather typical. Epiphora can appear either in the next line or at the end of the first and the third, or of the second and the fourth lines. Contrast serves a twofold purpose: first, it is a stylistic device for placing emphasis or conveying an emotional impression; secondly, it facilitates the grouping of four-verse stanzas, because the quatrain is the most popular form in Latvian folk literature. Usually, the first part of a stanza depicts an appropriate natural phenomenon, while the second part confronts it with human deeds or qualities.

Whereas legend describes some definite hero, event, or place, when these characteristics are omitted by storytellers, the narrative may adopt the form of a fairy tale. Monsters, wizards and witches are not popular in Latvian folklore. Instead, there are thousands of fine fairy tales portraying animals at their constructive work. The fox is most clever of the animals; the clumsy bear is great only in his physical strength, and the hare is consistently a coward. Giants, strongmen, and kings do exist; however, peasants and shepherds possess all the wisdom, as in "The King and the Sage":

> Once upon a time a king traveled over his domain to inspect it. Dusk fell as he returned to the palace; however, he surprised one of his subjects still at work.
> "You work rather hard," the king said. "What is your income?"
> "I earn eight Lats[1] a day, my king."
> "Whom do you support?"

[1] A monetary unit of Latvia, equal to 100 Santims.

"I contribute two Lats for the kingdom of God," the sage replied, "with two others I repay my debt; two Lats I deposit on interest, while the remaining money feeds my wife and myself."

The king was puzzled.

"Do you see, sir," the sage explained, "I support my ill brother, which I consider my contribution to God; the debt I am paying off I owe my father and my mother; by raising my children I make a good investment and the rest remains for us, old folks."

The king was proud of his subject.

(Aleksis Rubulis)

The character types are very explicit; they are either absolutely good or evil. Only an honest, struggling, and persecuted hero will be rewarded. God appears among people, and the deceitful but naive devil can be outwitted by a boy. Because of the common Indo-European origin or the migration of peoples, some Latvian fairy tales have international themes, although they have been localized to the Latvian mentality and surroundings.

Early Works

The oldest extant Latvian text is the Lord's Prayer quoted in the chronicle of the Dominican friar Simon Grunau between 1526 and 1531. However, other prayer texts must have been circulated earlier, for in 1198 Pope Innocent III ordered that Latvians be taught the Lord's Prayer, the manner of Confession, and the Creed. Heinricus de Lettis, who composed the *Heinrici Chronicon Lyvoniae* in 1225 and was a Latvian by birth, was instructed by papal legate William of Modena, later the Cardinal of Sabina, to translate twelve sacred, ecclesiastical texts which Latvians were to know by heart before they could be baptized. The same papal legate addressed the Latvian assembly around 1225. Biographers state that Erdmann Tolgsdorf introduced singing in St. Jacob's Church in Riga. The

Jesuit historian Alegamba mentions that Tolgsdorf composed Latvian church songs and sermons, and also compiled a dictionary. In all these cases there must have existed some patterns of Latvian writings, which perished when foreign troops, especially those of Ivan the Terrible, destroyed churches, libraries and archives, and devastated everything within reach.

According to K. L. Tetsch, there was seen in Sventaja a Lutheran handbook in two volumes, published in 1560. However, *Catechismus Catholicorum,* printed in Vilnius in 1585, is considered the first authentic book. The manuscript was prepared by Petrus Canisius. The Cēsis' annals of 1620 contain a biography of Tolgsdorf in which it is stated that he was the person who translated this catechism. In 1587 Luther's catechism (dated 1586) appeared, translated by Johannes Rivius and four other clergymen. This catechism, enlarged to include songs, epistles, and gospels, was named *Enchiridion* and printed in Königsberg.

After this a great number of publications appeared. The more significant ones were composed by the Lutheran pastor and scholar Georgius Mancelius: his handbook *Lettisch Vade mecum* (1631), the dictionary *Lettus* (1638), a selection of conversations, *Phraseologia Lettica* (1638), and the sermons *Lang-gewünschte Lettische Postill* (1654), which comprise 1200 pages rich in wit and biblical illustrations. Mancelius modernized the orthography. Juris Elģers, a Latvian Jesuit, translated *Religious Hymns* in 1621, Gospels in 1672, and a 674-page Polish-Latin-Latvian dictionary in 1683. Ernst Glück in cooperation with Jānis Reiters and Christophorus Füreccerus completed the translation of Luther's Bible. Another Latvian-born Jesuit and a professor at the Academy of Vilnius, Georgs Špungjanskis (1692–1733), published the grammar *Dispositio imperfecti ad optimum seu rudimenta grammatices lotavicae* (1732). The professor and Lutheran clergyman Gotthard Friedrich Stender compiled a larger grammar, *Neue vollständige lettische Grammatik* (1761), and the Jesuit Mikelis Rots published four books, among them translations from the Old and New Testaments.

National Literature

The foundation stone of independent national prose was laid by Juris Neikens (1826–1863), whose short stories deal with idealistic projects, family affairs, and prodigal sons. Juris Alunāns (1832–1864), after studying Roman, German, Russian, and Czech literature, created a national poetry supported by Krišjānis Barons (1835–1923), Fricis Brīvzemnieks (1846–1907), and Atis Kronvalds (1837–1875). Andrejs Pumpurs (1841–1902) reached outstanding heights in the national epic *Lāčplēsis;* ("bear-slayer"; 1888), based on legends and historical facts. Auseklis (1850–1879) emerged with several significant romantic lyrics, the finest among them "The Castle of Light," symbolizing the severe past of Latvia and predicting a bright future. Adolfs Alunāns (1848–1912), who composed dramas, trained actors, and organized performances across the country, is considered the father of the Latvian theater. Taking their material from the agrarian reform movement, two brothers, Reinis (1839–1920) and Matīss (1848–1926) Kaudzītes, jointly created the remarkable novel *The Times of Land-Surveyors* (1879), which portrays peasant life and is rich in wit.

Among the most popular realists were Jēkabs Janševskis (1865–1931), whose novel *The Native Land* (6 vols., 1924–1925) reveals great love of country and extols the virtue of labor, and Augusts Deglavs (1862–1922), author of the trilogy *Riga* (1912–1921). However, modern realism was first introduced in the nation by Rudolfs Blaumanis (1863–1908), grand master of the Latvian drama and short story. His style is terse; characters are endowed with courage and vigor. Blaumanis rejected Lombroso's theory of heredity and atavism as well as Dostoyevski's concept of environment; to the contrary, his heroes decide their own future and bear full responsibility for their actions. Blaumanis' attitude also contradicts Hippolyte A. Taine, French critic and professor of esthetics, who considered any work of art as a merely natural product, just as vitriol is.

For him, only three factors can determine art: time, race, and environment. Realism persisted in the works of Anna Brigadere (1861–1933) and Vilis Plūdonis (1874–1940), the greatest master of the modern ballad. Plūdonis wrote immortal verses about the ideals of youth, and their struggles to attain them. The poet proved his dexterity in all literary forms, concentrated his works to the maximum, constantly adjusted rhythm to the development and intensity of a plot, and adorned his works with metaphor and alliteration, achieving impressively picturesque and sonorous effects. Thus, his style in the translation of *Also sprach Zarathustra* is superior in quality to Nietzsche's original. The long poem *The Son of a Widow* (1900) plays the most important role among his numerous works, for it serves as a model for any diligent and persevering youth. In this work Plūdonis portrayed a young student who devises great plans for the future of his widowed mother and for mankind, as well. He is fully confident of being able to carry out his project:

> I want to climb the highest mountains,
> I feel quite strong, have fear of none;
> Let blizzards blow, let tempests thunder,
> But I will march still on and on!

Eventually, however, the boy's energy is exhausted; he is struck by illness and dies. Another masterpiece of Plūdonis is *The Requiem* (1899), which he dedicated to his dying brother.

The leading representative of romanticism is the dramatist and thinker, Jānis Rainis (1865–1929). Rainis, a jurist, visited many foreign countries and studied their political systems and literature, particularly the classics. After his return to Latvia, he attempted to implement social reforms; as a result, he was arrested in 1897 by the Russian militia. While in prison, the poet translated Goethe's *Faust;* however, his own works resemble Schiller's. He employed his genius in a struggle for truth, freedom, and beauty. Rainis' unique intellect and refined but vigorous expression mark all his numerous dramas. In the tragedy *Fire and Night* (1905), Rainis focuses on hostile forces and places them in conflict with the Latvian will to live and to sacrifice. The prototype Lāčplēsis ("bear-slayer," the national symbol of freedom), is offered a throne and treasure provided he will not resist the conquest of his native land. "My life is the future of my nation. Let it decide my fate!" he replies. And Spīdola ("radiance," representing women), encourages him: "Go and defeat our enemy, Lāčplēsis!" In the combat both Lāčplēsis and the Black Knight, who symbolizes the foreign invasion troops, fall off a cliff into the Daugava.[2] Spīdola rushes to aid her hero. Lāčplēsis and Spīdola exemplify the conformity of Latvian men and women to their traditional responsibility of making "Latvia beautiful and eternal." In 1921 the composer Jānis Mediņš (1890–1966) wrote an opera based on this tragedy.

When Bermont-Avalov endangered Riga, Rainis contributed the dramatic ballad *Daugava* (1919) which had enormous impact on the Latvian armed forces. Four thousand copies of the book were printed, but in less than two weeks it was out of print. Rainis' biblical tragedy, *Joseph and His Brothers* (1919), was published in many languages, including two English editions. His *chef-d'oeuvre,* "The Mountain Climber," taken from the collection of poems *Distant Feeling in a Blue Evening* (1903), reveals the poet's individuality, asceticism, and strong determination:

> Year after year your solitude will become stronger,
> For friends will quit and you must climb alone;
> Only rare soulmates will sight you sometimes
> And few sparse flowers growing on the stone.
>
> Then vanish even they. In the magnitude of mountains
> An endless tranquility will oppress your heart.
> You don't find peace among the dreadful fountains:
>
> The coldest glaciers will lie at your every turn,
> While in your bosom all the world's desire will burn.
>
> (Aleksis Rubulis)

---

[2] The greatest river in Latvia.

Many of Rainis' lyrics are intellectual. Contrary to those exemplified by the supermen Faust, Zarathustra, and Raskolnikov, the ideas of Rainis' Lāčplēsis, as well as of his other heroes, are carried out only through self-sacrifice. "The Sole Star," taken from *Distant Feeling in a Blue Evening,* merely divulges the poet's self-renunciation in favor of his goals and affirms the presence of fanaticism in the world, for any indignant act against mankind is contrary to the *Weltanschauung* of Rainis:

> An idea, if valued supreme,
> Doesn't comply with mercy.
>
> He whom its flame has seized
> Strives, except for survival.
>
> He sacrifices himself, each and all
> For the idea he worships.
>
> You can praise him, ignore or accuse;
> He will proceed unaffectedly.
>
> A pitch-dark shield arches his sight;
> All he spots and holds is his star.
>
> (Aleksis Rubulis)

Jānis Rainis recognized discord among men. He did not attempt to reconcile it; instead, the poet invigorated his heroes and set them against the wrong and evil-minded. Rainis' symbolic romanticism exposes the struggle between opposing ideologies and, therefore, his character portrayal is somewhat deficient: his individuals are confident of their beliefs and tasks; they bear scarcely a trace of nuance or gradation of personality. Their love is inflexibly animistic; no physical glamour can enrapture them. In regard to literary genres, Rainis stated: "Poetry is the sun that animates quickly; prose is the moon that shapes slowly; aphorism is the thunderbolt that illuminates everything at once."

Jānis Rainis participated in the 1905 revolution and, consequently, had to escape to Switzerland, where he lived until 1920. From 1926 until 1928 he was a Minister of Education in Latvia.

Rainis translated into Latvian Shakespeare's *King Lear* and *Antony and Cleopatra,* Pushkin's *Boris Godunov,* and Schiller's *Wilhelm Tell.* His own works exceed twenty volumes.

Influenced by the philosophies of Plato and Kant and by Wagner's operas, Jānis Poruks (1871–1911) wrote highly refined and sensitive lyrics that rank among those of the best European romanticists. All of his works sound best when read to melancholy, somber melodies. His symbolic narrative *The Fisher of Pearls* (1895) reveals the author's character and is a wonderful song of tribute to any searcher of pure heart and mind. The impressionist Fricis Bārda (1880–1919) constantly searched for comfort in an idealized world. His philosophical lyrics are impregnated with pensive melancholy.

Neoromanticist Jānis Akurāters (1876–1939) advocated the supremacy of intellect in the novel *Pēteris Danga* (1921). Another novel, *The Fiery Flowers* (1925), is based on the author's biography. Akurāters also wrote twelve volumes of hymnic and enthusiastic lyrics, impressionistic short stories, and plays which are more realistic.

Besides twelve volumes of poetry and some threescore stories, the individualistic romanticist Kārlis Skalbe (b. 1879; died 1945 in Stockholm) produced seventy-six fairy tales, which are included in the ten volumes of his *Works* (1938–1939) and rank with the best of the fairy tales of Hans Christian Andersen and Oscar Wilde. His typical hero is the *rex dolorosus* who is endowed with humanity, philanthropy, and often cosmopolitanism. For example, in one of his tales a giant discovers his vocation in holding a mountain on his back. "His life was fulfilled and joyful," for thus he preserved trees, birds, and flowers. Because Skalbe employs allegory, adults find in his works profound philosophical and esthetical values. Only "My Voyage to the North Maiden" (1904) contains subtle irony. It was Skalbe's reply to a tale by Andrievs Niedra (1871–1942) entitled *The Farmer's Son* (1902), in which a youngster discontented with mental gifts begins to hanker for material goods. "My Voyage to the North Maiden" is presented below in an abridged form:

All around me billows howled like greedy wolves, and my ship cruelly stroked their white and sulky backs. Some reared and gaped their foamy jaws in a wild roar, attempting to crush my ship; the Young Strength, however, cut the green jaws and proudly sailed forward.

On the horizon strange white icebergs came into sight, for there the kingdom of the North Maiden began. The icebergs proved to be her giants, who had decided to wrestle in the vast sea. I saw how they charged each other, brandishing hundreds of glittering ice swords, then thronged into a huge mountain and with a horrifying sound burst into pieces and dispersed all over the sea. Many a floe passed my ship, rubbing its belly against her sides.

Finally, I stood at the gates of the North Kingdom. On both sides ice giants towered, holding their swords ready. From their midst wound a cleft, in which melted icebrains surged. Across the cleft a Sea Giant lay like a long, dark island. His broad face sank in the water and his swollen, half-closed eyes shone like the fire in an oven through a door-slit, while his nostrils spouted jets of fire and smoke. My ship fearlessly rushed along the ice raft toward a monster. One of the giants approached me clumsily. Young Strength, however, thrust out its oaken chest and hurled its sharp forehead into his flank. Within an instant the giant started to stagger, and soon he collapsed. I don't remember how long my journey continued, but the ship crashed on rocks. In despair I looked at the broken spar and noticed a strip of land. I launched a boat and set forth.

Advancing toward the coast, I discerned something strange. Up to now the horizon remained far from me, no matter how I tried to reach it. My objective was visible only in the distance, which made it beautiful. But now I recognized that with every minute it came closer and closer. On the shore I saw that the sky met the earth like a grey wall, and chimneys had covered its edge with soot.

Then I heard voices and, raising my head, saw fat people with ruddy faces who wore soft coats. They inquired about me with compassion, and I related my adventures to them as if in a dream. I had the impression that they already knew my experiences and listened to my story only to affirm their conviction. In my misfortune they searched for their own justification, found it and rejoiced. Their voyage had brought them to the Country of Peace and Prosperity, where only rest and happiness exist. "The idealism of youth! . . . Fervent blood. . . . Fantastic dreams. . . ." they spoke in chorus while I sat on a rock in sorrow.

"Goodheart, Goodheart!" they whispered, and soon someone patted my shoulder. I perceived an old round face, a round stomach, and soft, round fingers.

"Don't worry!" Goodheart said, "the life is good here. Look, all of us have put on flesh." He gave a wink and glanced over his subjects. "I have helped them. I love young people and enjoy their success. Cheer up! I shall supply you with plenty of meat. Go, take as much sauerkraut from the barrel as you want. My daughter, Beetle, will cook it for you. You have arrived just before our great festivity: today we are celebrating the killing of hogs. Let's go! Be our guest."

They removed me from the rock and drove me forcibly toward their dwelling. Before it, long tables were placed. Hot steam rolled through the open door. From the kitchen to the court, from the court to the kitchen, florid girls walked, carrying one dish after another.

"The banquet is ready," Goodheart cried jovially. "Let's enjoy it!"

All sat at the tables. I followed suit.

How low, how low was their sky! Near every eater a spoon was stuck in the sky, but over my head a steelyard also hung down. People seized their spoons from the sky, and started to eat. I also tried to partake, but the meal didn't have any taste and I hid my spoon under the bowl.

Goodheart noticed it. "Oh," he wondered, "you are not accustomed to our favorite dish! Beetle, offer our guest honey!"

A round, dark girl rose up and handed me a large pot of honey and a huge jug of milk. "You can eat more honey, if you wash it down with milk," she instructed me lovingly. Bread crumbs clung to the corners of her mouth, and a drop of honey shone in her dimple.

When the champing and puffing ceased, one of the men announced his speech by knocking a gnawed pig-bone against his bowl. Everyone grew silent.

Goodheart whispered to me, "It's our prophet, Paunchy."

"Ladies and gentlemen," Paunchy began, "the time has arrived in the Country of Peace and Prosperity when we can celebrate our traditional killing of hogs. The largest hog has been butchered, and from every bowl its fat flesh smiles at us. Grease shines on everyone's lips, and all cheeks express joy and happiness. Let's clarify who deserves our gratitude. Ancient Greeks had already discovered that a warm fog which enfolds our land contributes significantly to the fattening of pigs; in our time every child knows that the fog is the source of our prosperity. Who maintains this fog? It is our low sky, which impedes its passage. And we must thank our sky for peace also. There is no need for us to look afar. Our horizon ends before our very eyes; it is within the reach of our hands. This is exceptionally practical, and no mortal can desire more. We can obtain all daily necessities without a single motion."

"Our prophet spoke well," they acknowledged, "just as he did last year and the year before that."

Thus I lived in the Country of Peace and Prosperity or the Country of Fat Hogs, as it was nicknamed. I had been granted all privileges, but people wondered why I didn't grow fat.

Frequently Beetle visited me. Every time she brought milk and honey.

"Get up and drink," she said with affection, "then you will be able to eat more."

I looked at her and felt sorry for her. She was good and lovely, but still far from me, far from all that I held in my bosom.

"Why do they call you Beetle?" I asked in grief and anger. "You are a human being. Who dares to mistake a human being for an insect!"

"Don't you like my name?" She opened her eyes in surprise. "My daddy loves it. He says that I am as round as a beetle," she swung around on her heel. "Someday the whole earth will become even, and people will roll over it like balls. The time will come when there will be no need to get up or pace; we'll walk while sleeping. Only round people are beautiful. Daddy says that you must improve. Now you resemble a board. Ha, ha, ha. . . ."

Laima[3] took pity on me, granting me a vision. The air was filled with something pure and gentle. It was evident that someone great and holy was near me. I raised my head: the North Maiden was with me! I recognized her at once. Her eyes shone with a radiance that could enkindle the sky. From her blushing features clouds turned purple, and water glittered like gold.

"I know you have been longing for me," she said, "and I came to rescue you."

Then she put her hand on my heart and voiced the tragic fact: "The fog has squeezed it flat."

The North Maiden breathed upon me. At that instant I felt something expand in my bosom, and big tears ran over my cheeks.

"Weep away all rubbish from your heart to make it pure again," she advised, and after a while continued, "I will endow it with favor. Be it so! Now you are strong. Come, I shall show you my sky."

She led me upwards. We ascended the purple mountains of clouds, where the atmosphere glowed with her presence. There we met the Morning Star.

"Where are you rushing?" the North Maiden asked.

"I am on my way to light the swamp. Two children went astray there in their search for the sky. I must show them the road."

"Stars are my friends," the North Maiden explained, and moved on as brightly as the sun.

We approached a huge mountain of clouds which quaked and rumbled. Soon I saw three beehives.[4] The bees' strong gloved hands turned millstones. The creatures had big heads, and they wore icicles instead of beards.

[3] A goddess in Latvian mythology. In the Middle Ages her name became associated with the Virgin Mary.

[4] Bees are considered a symbol of diligence in the Latvian folklore.

"They are our millers of snow," the North Maiden confided. "Look down!"

I saw a muddy space and a beggar wading in it. Snowflakes gently covered all.

"The earth is dirty," the North Maiden stated softly.

"Let me turn the millstones!" I called eagerly.

"You have another task," she smiled. "Follow me."

Then she pointed to the path leading across a mountain range. A bright light illuminated it. Out of the dark ravines soiled people climbed upwards and, having cleansed themselves, went their way. Again I sensed something great and holy. The North Maiden kissed me, and I arose. I jumped up and shouted:

"Get up! Wake up!"

The fog vibrated with my shrill sound, and the soot poured upon my head. Soon the door squeaked, and a dull red-faced guard commanded, "Let's go! The supreme court wants you."

Paunchy glanced at the records and stated:

"Young man, you are accused of disturbance of the peace on the night of the twenty-fourth sleeping month. The alarm agitated the whole vicinity, with the result that our people couldn't rest calmly for several nights. You have violated the most sacred law of our country, man's right to sleep, committing a most serious crime. What do you have to say in your defense?"

"I am glad they had a chance to open their eyes."

"You are fresh. I sentence you to go down on your knees, to humiliate yourself before our people, and to repent your offence; otherwise, you will be banished."

"I would break all chains to get out of here," I replied.

I embarked on my ship anew. By day the sun embraced me with gold, and the stars guided me at night. I looked at the remote distance and thought, "The world has no end, and the sky has no edge. A true life is as great as the world and as high as the sky."

(Aleksis Rubulis)

The Latvian literary giant differs from his foreign colleagues. To Wilde, "There is no such thing as a moral or immoral book.

Books are well written, or badly written. That is all." He judged
a book's worth by the criteria of beauty and fascination alone.
Andersen, on the other hand, aspired after luster and frolic-
some episodes and treated them with satire. Kārlis Skalbe, called
the King of Fairy Tales, can be compared with St. Francis of
Assisi, who called all creatures his brothers and sisters. This is
due to his nature, as well as to the fact that Skalbe drew his
material from the inexhaustible reservoir of Latvian folklore.
All his animals, plants, and even water are animated and delineated with gentleness and respect. The fairy tale "The Poor
Brahman" contains a distinctive example: "A picked lotus
flower is beautiful, but it is more elegant while swaying in a
whirlpool." Skalbe places emphasis on moral philosophy. Although the happy ending is typical of his works, he often
depicts heroes who are willing to sacrifice their lives or give up
fortune to retain their integrity and virtue:

The Contented Fisherman

Jurgis was a fisherman. His small house with a reed roof
overgrown with moss stood on the bank of a river. In front
of his door grew an old willow with wide branches, on which
Jurgis used to dry his nets. On the threshold a cat often
sunned itself, and in a window geraniums blossomed. Every
time the fisherman returned home the cat, scenting fish,
rubbed against his feet. Then his wife approached from the
hearth and, taking the wet bag from his shoulders, caressed
him. She had an expressive face which was sad and wrinkled.
She always complained of being ill, but every task was done
and all the clothes were mended and patched. His flaxen-
haired son and daughter rushed to meet their father and with
their hands pulled shiny fish out of the bag. Perhaps it was
boring to live at the very edge of the forest. Whenever Jurgis stepped out to get a breath of fresh air, the old willow
whimpered in the wind as if complaining of the heavy nets.
And Jurgis also gave a deep sigh.

The fate of Jurgis depended upon the river, which slowly
wound along the red sand and only at places formed coves
and whirlpools. The fisherman loved the river like his own

mother. He also pleaded with it and cursed it, for his river
was lazy and miserly. Seldom could he land a few stout tench
or a sizable pike. Roach, carp, flounder, and perch were his
usual catch. The fisherman had to work hard to support his
wife and children. He never spared his energy. Before dawn,
when stars still twinkled in the sky and dark waters murmured against the shore, he set out to fish. For hours and
hours he rowed his boat, casting nets, and only during the
noontide heat would he lay down the oars and relax from
time to time. Reeds rustled gently in the breeze as if singing
a lullaby; he rested under the open sky and felt as if he were
in the cradle of God. Aroused, he seized the oars again. And
the river did not disappoint him. Indeed, at times the catch
was poor. One evening he brought home only five flounder.

"Oh dear!" his wife complained. "Flounder again."

"Well, it's still fish," Jurgis replied. He believed in hard
work and refused to admit his failure.

His wife baked the fish on charcoal, and the whole family
ate it with salt and bread.

"You see," Jurgis remarked, "it was enough for supper.
Tomorrow, with God's help, we'll have more."

"It would be nice to get more, dear," his wife added bit-
terly. "Look, the girl needs shoes. And our boy doesn't have
a hat."

"Who needs a hat in summer!" Jurgis looked for an
excuse, patting his son on the head with the rough palm of
his hand.

His wife bent her head and watched the dying fire.

The fisherman went out. The night was calm; only the old
willow whimpered in the wind.

"It whimpers and complains," Jurgis sighed reproachfully
and retired to bed.

Next morning he put the net on his shoulders and set out
for the river. "You work and worry but achieve nothing!"
the man exclaimed. He cursed his life and his home where
there was nothing but misery; he cursed even his wife who
was neither healthy nor sick. He cast the net several times
but in vain. "The deuce take such a life!" he snapped.

Suddenly he noticed that the net became unusually heavy.

The fisherman couldn't comprehend what had happened. He saw two large black eyes peering at him from the water. "Talk of the devil and he is sure to appear," Jurgis, startled, uttered the bitter truth.

"Pull me out of this whirlpool," the devil pleaded, "and I shall give you everything you want: a lot of money, a lovely wife, a beautiful castle, a horse with a cart, and many servants."

"What a lord you are! Can't you get out by yourself?"

"No. I am bound to the bottom of the river."

Jurgis didn't have to be told twice. He grabbed the net with tremendous force to draw closer those eyes which promised to fulfill all his desires. He twisted and dragged the ropes, and all the dark depths rose up. Huge billows towered all around. Suddenly he realized that his boat was moving beside his house. The walls of the house cracked, a strong wind blew every window open and overturned the geraniums. His wife was horrified. "My God!" Jurgis exclaimed and made the sign of the cross. The bewildering eyes vanished, and the waves ceased and disappeared. On the instant, Jurgis appeared at home and embraced his wife and his children. The fisherman was now joyful in spite of his poverty. Never before had he realized that he loved his simple and poor life.

(Aleksis Rubulis)

A wide geographical spectrum fashions the background for the works of Jānis Jaunsudrabiņš (1877–1962), whose contribution is twofold: literature and painting. In 1908 he set off to Berlin to study art under Lovis Corinth (1858–1925), the leading German impressionist. Jaunsudrabiņš' exhibitions of paintings which adhered to tradition gained recognition in Latvia and abroad. In literature, however, he started with impressionism and then switched to realism. In his trilogy: *Aija* (1911), *Echo* (1914), and *Winter* (1924) and in the novels *The Death Dance* (1924), *The Settler and the Devil* (1933), *Don't Look at the Sun* (1936), and *Money* (1942), he unfolded the lives of whimsical, depraved women, and corresponding male characters in social entanglements. Jaunsudrabiņš' heroes are common people; his language is naturally simple and is interlaced with provincialisms. The narratives *Caucasus* (1920) and *Capri* (1939) embody reflections of his sentiments. He often refers to the sun, both in realistic and in symbolic terms. One of his paintings shows the sun in all its golden radiance.

Jaunsudrabiņš was a man of integrity, and despised any pretense. He was an ardent angler and loved to spend his leisure at the seaside or lakeshore. His splendid narrative *Waters* (1921) is a song of tribute to the wonderful harmony of nature and a testament of the author's profound love for it: "The trees, the flowers, the earth, the air, everything living and lifeless, we are one body and one soul. The fact that the vibration of my brain is wider, makes wider the world of my feelings—in everything else I am similar to that tree in whose shadow I am sitting, and to that innocent bird which looks at me without fear when I do not lift my hand against it." Jaunsudrabiņš' works comprise seven novels, about thirty volumes of short stories, and eleven plays.

Edvards Virza (1883–1940) made his debut with a sensual portrayal of glamorous physique in the collection of poetry *The Cup* (1908). His evident decadence differs from that of Verlaine, Baudelaire, and Oscar Wilde in this respect: he saw no beauty in decay nor did he glory in attacking society. Rather, Virza's decadence stems from his unceasing research and extreme refinement, which is similar to that of Arthur Symons. His next collection, *The Divine Game* (1919), is marked with temperance and erudition; eroticism, however, is present also in the poet's later lyrics. Virza appropriated both his energetic rhythm and his fantasy from the Belgian mystic-naturalist Emile Verhaeren, whose selected works, *The Feature of Life*, he translated in 1920. Virza introduced to Latvian literature other esthetic devices influenced by his contact with French literary schools, for in 1921 he moved to Paris, where he worked for some time at the Latvian legation. French symbolic, Parnassian, and romantic lyrics were rendered into Latvian in his *French Poetry in the Nineteenth Century* (1921), and his *Lyrics of the French Renaissance* appeared in 1930.

Frequently Virza chose national themes. His *Poems* (1924) contains the historical epics "King Namejs" and "Duke Jēkabs," executed in the heroic Alexandrine verse. He accumulated material for his poetry from episodes of great valor and rendered those episodes with resonant, brazen sound. A Lutheran himself, Virza wrote a few Catholic church hymns. In his prose, however, ancient pagan traditions dominate sparse Christian glimpses. The style is exalted; at times it is solemnly biblical. Virza's capital work is the novel *Straumēni* (1933), which pictures a patriarchal farmstead within the four seasons. Virza called the work a poem because of its obvious token of rhythm and because he chose for his subject the farmstead *Straumēni* rather than a human as in the traditional Latvian novel. The excerpt depicts ancient heathen superstitions blended with Christianity:

At Straumēni people celebrated the feast of St. John with great splendor, for the master himself was called Jānis. Provisions were so plentiful that everyone long remembered those days. This feast pleased the master especially, for he could go to some expense celebrating with his friends and his servants. Of course, this holiday pleased everyone because labor in the fields stood as if in abeyance and the laborers were preparing to take back from the fields and meadows what they had earlier put into them.

On the Saturday of the feast of St. John, work stopped at Straumēni about noon. The youngest hands, astride the horses, took them bathing in the stream. Naked atop the animals, they made them turn around and around in the water, and the horses neighed with pleasure as the whirling stream cleansed their coats of all the summer's dust and sweat. Back on the bank, their black and brown coats glistening, they seemed to be the very horses with which John[5] traverses the fields of Zemgale.[6]

The mistress of Straumēni had long since been ready for this day, and the cellar doors were now wide open. Gold as

[5] Jānis (in English, John) is enveloped by Christian as well as ancient heathen traditions, and, therefore, he frequently bears mysterious characteristics.

[6] A province of Latvia.

the autumn sun, the cheeses of St. John, wrapped in white muslin, were taken to the granary together with pots of butter and smoked hams. Big oak branches, like those whose lacy leaves entwine on carved bedsteads, had already been hung about. Their dark green color blended into the half-light of the room, and only the freshness emanating from them indicated that they were alive. Heaped in a sieve, still steaming with the oven's heat, revealing crisp bacon through clefts in their sides, the small pasties were brought in and piled onto plates on the table. There they joined the brandy in brown earthen jugs and the beer in the oaken pitchers made long ago by the grandfather. In a corner of the granary, on a little table, stood a keg of beer bound with wooden hoops, a tap below to facilitate the drawing of the juice of barley and hops, that old inflamer of heads, whose pleasure it is to make men dance. Also gracing the table were bottles of sweetened brandy flavored with aniseed or berries, and when it was poured into the glasses it trickled out, thick as honey fresh from the combs. The master himself had made it the preceding summer, distilling and filtering until, enclosed in bottles sealed with wax and exposed for long months to the sun, it had flowered and ripened to become like fruit.

Around the door frames heavy oak wreaths had been hung on nails driven in long ago, and in front of the granary older women sat in the grass and plaited more. In the woodshed Janka[7] was fussing around three old wagon-wheel hubs, filling them with resinous wood which he had saved since winter for today's celebration. Everything had to be ready on time, for the neighbors were used to arriving at Straumēni around tea time on St. John's eve.

The first to arrive in the barnyard was the nearest neighbor, the farmer of Puravelni, a tall and robust man, clenching a long-stemmed pipe in his teeth. He was barefooted in his wooden shoes, his jacket and shirt were open in front, and across his tanned and bulging chest the muscles played and rippled like ropes. He was always bare-chested even in winter when he wore his fur jacket. He considered clothes an insupportable burden. In the sharpest frost his feet were bare in

---

[7] The diminutive of Jānis, "Johnny."

his wooden shoes, and the cold seemed powerless against him. He liked to sleep in the granary until the first snow and, in autumn, as the grains were stored leaving no room for a bed, he slept in the bins on the wheat or the rye. Authoritarian and tyrannical by nature, he often quarreled with others, for he was fond of jests, and in his speech he liked to lay traps for his companions, which irritated them. He particularly hated gypsies, and one day when he had caught a gypsy girl in his woods he tied her to a birch by her hair and fired blank charges at her. After that, the gypsies took wide detours to avoid his house. He managed his 300 *pūrvietas*[8] of land with a great skill.

The two farmers had just finished their third glass when three carriages with green painted springs, each drawn by two horses, entered the barnyard. In the first were the Bitenieks, a farmer and his wife from a neighboring township. He was the greatest horse-fancier in the district. Anyone seeing a cloud of dust swirling along the main road knew that Bitenieks' wagon was not far ahead. Once he had careened right under the porch of the church with his black horses, pretending he could not control them. Bitenieks was a haughty man, rather impulsive, who liked to stop at all the inns and pay for a round of brandy and beer and then drive on.

The next guest, the farmer Billis, was a thin man with a dark face who liked to say that he was of Turkish blood. He was not as good a farmer as the others, for his interests ran in other directions. He liked to learn, know, listen. In town or elsewhere he sought the company of a variety of people, asking about everything; that is why his memory, which let nothing escape, was filled with myriad wars, generals, sovereigns, and the ancient rulers of Kurzeme.[9] Above all he enjoyed drinking with friends, introducing into the conversation his yarns, which he liked to spin while pacing back and forth in the room, tamping the tobacco in his short pipe with his thumb.

The farmer of Daukni was the last to arrive, as was proper

[8] A *pūrvieta* equals about an acre.
[9] The western province of Latvia.

for the most important among the friends of Straumēni. He was a tall man with wide shoulders, somewhat stooped, and wore long, drooping mustaches like those affected by Polish noblemen. His graying hair, parted in the center, fell to his shoulders. He was rather haughty by nature, liked no one in particular, yet everyone willingly listened to him. He judged calmly and, with no effort at all, managed to dominate everyone.

These guests alighted in the barnyard of Straumēni on the feast of St. John, the men carrying bottles in their pockets and the women clutching cheeses in their kerchiefs. All these gifts, accompanied by good wishes, were handed to the farmer and his wife. The farmyard suddenly echoed with joyful talk as one and all, after shaking the dust from their clothes, went to the storehouse to feast St. John's eve. They stopped halfway, to look at each other, for they had not seen each other since Christmas. Now their faces were tanned by the sun, and as they had known one another since childhood, they did not try to put on airs.

In the granary the conversations immediately turned to the work of the fields, and all the events concerning the harvests and the flocks were passed in review. Although they were rich farmers, unaccustomed to defer to anyone, they relied on the protection of God as little children confide in their mothers. He guided them through life with his steady Hand, as he had guided their fathers before them, and the most unfortunate was he who broke free from the divine grasp. Soon the power of the barley and hops, in which God's spirit surely dwells also, hovered over the room, and the scolloped green branches seemed to be wreaths on the heads of the merrymakers. The conversations of the people of this district, whether they had drunk or not, took on a strange character. In their talk they tried to find one another's weak point, which obliged them to keep on the defensive, and the conversations inevitably turned into duels of jesting. To look at them, you would have thought you saw together the most rabid enemies, even though they were united by the closest bonds of kinship and friendship.

During this time other guests were arriving and everyone

went out to meet them. The farmyard was now filled with people. There were farmers in gray or black suits, their wives in full skirts and wearing bonnets. Work and the rich earth had made them well-to-do. The Lielupe,[10] which exhaled a humid breath over their fields in the summer and in the spring flooded them with silty water, was their foster-mother. With the same slowness with which she flowed toward the sea, they proceeded through life, for the heavy earth on which they grew up had taken all haste from their steps. The sun was going down in the west and the rising dust grew red over the herd hurrying back to the farm. The cows, pressed together in the narrow lane, clashed horns, and one could see the sheen of their smooth croups. All had swollen udders, and, as they ran by, an odor of milk pervaded the air. The milkmaids, that evening, were quick about taking care of the cows; then, after changing, they joined the others, all of whom had oak leaf crowns on their heads. The assembly, singing the songs of St. John's day, walked up the hill behind the house where, at that moment, the men were finishing the job of attaching the wood-filled wheel hubs to the tops of posts. The master himself set them afire, and when they were raised up, three bouquets of red and smoky flames rose straight to the sky. The songs of *līgo* swelled with renewed vigor. Just as in the springtime the plow and other tools are brought from the shed to enter into service, so these hymns, which all year long had remained dormant in the memory, sprang out that night to resound over the same meadows and fields whose spirit had inspired them. Fires flared also near other farms; their light shone through or above groves of trees, and soon the entire countryside was studded with flames which lit up the fields of rye, wheat, oats, and barley. These lights frightened the rails which, hidden in the thickest growth of the grains, contemplated them in silence for a moment and then ran to the middle of the fields repeating their mournful calls. The entire horizon was filled with fires, and song welled up from every farm in the district.

The keg of beer which had been set up near the Straumēni fires was already half empty, and everyone sang and talked in

10 A river in Zemgale.

the greatest confusion. As for the farmer of Puravelni, foam not only covered his beard, but flowered upon the foliage of his wreath. Enormous, bare-chested, he seemed to be John himself, sweeping the company along in unbridled cheer. One of the burning casks was almost out; another was brought to replace it, and Kārlis, to whom the beer imparted the strength of Hercules, got the idea of hoisting the cask to the top of a birch which had been struck by lightning but retained its green life, if little of its bark. Up in the branches, he attached his belt to the cask, slung it over his shoulder, and began to climb still higher. Gathered around the tree the guests followed him with their eyes, singing and uttering cries of triumph. Kārlis disappeared for a moment and the onlookers caught sight of him only when the fire, being lit, appeared above the top of the birch tree. Soon it rose to the tip of the pole which Kārlis tied securely to the tree top. Although there was not the slightest breeze, the flames at that height leaned to one side, and since, especially from a distance, one could not see the pole supporting the firework, it seemed to be suspended in the air like an immense star.

When Kārlis reached the ground he was greeted with joyous exclamations, with praise, and he was obliged to down a full pitcher of beer in one draft. Old Janka approached him and said, "If I had had the money, I would have bet a pint of brandy that you couldn't have hoisted the cask!"

The fire, burning at the height of a church tower, could be seen throughout the district, and the chants at the other farms were stilled for a moment while the singers contemplated this extraordinary sight. The brazier on high roared like spring waters in the ditches, and sparks flew across the fields as far as half a kilometer away. The stalks of grain seemed to awaken and gaze in wonder at the crackling fire burning in the sky. Crossing the meadows and the edges of the fields, a troop of neighbors arrived singing, crowned with wreaths, and carrying bouquets of wild flowers. How could one tell whether the girls' faces were red because of the fire or because of the songs? The songs of the older women, today, brought to light everything that they usually kept under cover—those songs which have the immodest innocence of the wild plants, flowers, creatures, harvests.

The cask had burned itself out, flaming sticks dropped from it, showering the birch tree with sparks. Only the pole with its glowing red clamps remained, and the troop of singers went back to the granary to begin the feasting of St. John's eve in earnest. Right from the oven there came a platter of lamb with its thick cream sauce and onions, accompanied by golden potatoes and crisp, fat pork ribs. In saucers there were the huckleberry jam and the cucumbers, which, though pickled last autumn, had kept their firmness. Set crosswise on the table was a baked pike so large that when Kārlis had caught it he had nearly been knocked over by a flip of its tail. At this point the farmer uncorked bottles of herb brandy, and when the guests turned their glasses bottoms up they had the sensation of swallowing flavored fire. Since the lamplight was too weak, they brought from the house thin slats that smoked while burning and left long twisted chars at their tips as they burned down. In this subdued light the oak leaves seemed even greener. At first everyone ate in silence, flinging to the floor bones which the dogs noisily grabbed. Harassed by the dogs, the cat took refuge on a shelf, where his green eyes peered about the room all the while he washed his face. Little by little the tongues were loosened, and the pitch rose to such a point that the clatter of the dishes was no longer heard. The good humor increased when the farmer of Puravelni, forgetting that his stool had no back, felt the need to relax and fell over backwards. There was such a roar that the ferret, who lurked in the foundations of the storehouse and had for a long time been listening, terrified, to the hubbub above her, fled worriedly with her babies to find a sleeping place in the nettles growing around the edges of the farmyard.

Soon, personal fantasies peopled the head of each reveler, and, becoming absorbed in them, he spoke without hearing what the others were saying. The conversations now brought to mind those hobbled horses that can make progress only by short hops. Each saw the faces of the others as through a thick fog, and their minds flitted about in their own fantasies like quail in a wheat field.

A heavy warmth had accumulated in the room and the low doors could not let out the suffocating heat which rose from the food, the lamps, and from all these men whose foreheads gleamed with fat drops of sweat. Some took off their jackets; others, knocking their heads against the door lintels, went into the yard where the people, there too, were growing tired of dancing to the tunes played without intermission by old man Knabens. Half-blinded by the thick wreaths which kept falling over their eyes, men, women, and lasses were swirling and tapping out the rhythm, and not a soul caught sight of the first swallow which, flying from its nest and twittering happily, went swooping over the barnyard.

Here and there near a few farms, one could see lingering bonfires flaming feebly, red in the pale light of the morning. The last burning sticks were dropping from them, and the blackened poles stood upright in charred solitude. The singers had become silent. Only the footprints they had left upon the meadows wet with dew bore witness to the evening gaiety. The web of their prints crisscrossed from one farm to the other like narrow green carpets that one had forgotten to roll up after the passing of a procession.

The farmhands of Straumēni had hitched up the visitors' horses and led them into the yard. It was difficult to control them, for all night long they had rested and gorged themselves with fodder. Saying good-bye for the third time around, those leaving and those remaining shook hands, and only after emptying the last glass did the guests climb into their carriages and drive away, still crowned with wreaths. The horses began to trot right away, and the people of Straumēni long heard the jingling of the bells attached to the bow of the shafts. It seemed to them as if John himself, drunk with wine and cheer, were returning to his abode beyond the sun.

(Charles F. Roedig)

A strong expressionsim dominated the early works of Jānis Ezeriņš (1891–1924), but later he vacillated between realism and romanticism. Ezeriņš attracted a wide audience with his psychological short stories in *The Bard and Devil* (1920), *In the Barracks of His Majesty* (1922), *The Fantastic Story and Others* (1922), and *The Street-Organ* (Vol. I, 1923; Vol. II, 1925), in which he utilized a terse and intriguing style which he had derived from his studies of the works of Maupassant, Poe, and Wilde.

During the period of independence many literati hailed the cultural and economic progress. A poem of Jonass Miesnieks (b. 1896; now living in Philadelphia), set to music by Jānis Norvilis, became a national hit:

The Voices

The voices, the voices, they thrill me and charm:
all skylarks resound them in heaven,
high mountains re-echo, green forests sough forth,
and ploughmen and shepherds respond t'them.

These voices urge women and men to get up,
thank God for the beautiful sunrise
and, blessing our labor at homes and in fields,
let Latvia flourish and prosper.

(Aleksis Rubulis)

Jonass Miesnieks pictured family affairs in the novel *The Portrait of Bērzups' Family* (1935) and historical events of the sixteenth century in *The Judge of the Livonian District* (1948). He also wrote short stories. From 1931 to 1940, Miesnieks served as a judge.

The best known Latvian writer abroad is Zenta Mauriņa (b. 1897; now in Germany). She was the first woman to obtain a Ph.D. from the University of Latvia (1937). Afterwards she pursued postgraduate studies in Vienna, Paris, Florence, and Heidelberg. Her contribution embraces two genres, the essay and fiction. In the books of essays *Principal Motifs in the Art of Rainis* (1928), *Jānis Poruks and Romanticism* (1929), *Dostoyevski* (1929), *In the Light of Prometheus* (1942), *Dante* (1952), *The Meeting with Elly Ney* (1956), *International Unity and the Task of the Individual* (1963), *The Responsibility of a Poet in Our Time* (1965), and many more, the author primarily interprets various philosophical conflicts and searches for a solution through the intellect and through love. Being unusually well-read, she is competent to analyze the works and ideas of many nations and schools of thought.

Zenta Mauriņa has produced numerous novels, such as *In the Train of Life* (1941), *Three Brothers* (1946), *Francesca* (1952), the autobiographical trilogy *The Far Journey* (1951), *To Venture Is Beautiful* (1953), and *The Iron Bolts Break* (1957), the collections of short stories *Seven Guests* (1961) and *Birchbark* (1967), from which the excerpt below is taken. The translator provides the following introduction to the excerpt:

Young Ruth has traveled a great distance—some six thousand kilometers or more—from her home in Riga straight across the vast windswept stretches of Siberia to where the Amur River flows into the Sea of Okhotsk in order to visit her former teacher, the poet Janis Sarma, a man who was the idol of her schoolgirl dreams and reveries but whom she has not seen in more than fifteen years. Because of his "counterrevolutionary" poetry, redolent of his yearnings and demands for personal as well as political freedom, Janis Sarma had been condemned to ten years imprisonment in a Siberian labor camp. Forbidden to return again to his homeland after the expiration of his prison term, he settled down alone in a little secluded shack in the Siberian taiga. One evening now, the two of them, Ruth and the prematurely aging poet, sitting until late into the night on the doorstep of his miserable shack, relate to one another the fates of their friends and of those who had been their enemies, people the paths of whose lives had in the past momentarily crossed, affecting one another at times for the good and yet, at other times, in part contradicting themselves as well.

Ruth had told him all these things without stopping once, just as one is wont to narrate things which he has repeated to himself countless times, things which he has memorized by heart without ever having had the chance to share them with someone else. Then, after a moment, Janis said, pensively and almost as if speaking to himself:

"Thymiane, the harpist from Berlin, oh yes, I knew her, or I should say, I was together with her a few times, but each meeting has remained something unforgettable for me. She was a woman of rare fascination.

"Once I was walking with her along the seashore when suddenly she asked me, 'Have you ever seen a water nymph?' She threw her head back and shook her long brown hair almost as if it were a flowing mane, flooding me all the while with the radiance of her eyes, with their fairylike beauty and their long black lashes.

" 'O yes,' I replied, 'I've seen many of them, dozens of them in fact.' She laughed and her voice sounded just like the melodious tones of her harp. 'Maybe, but your water nymphs live only in poetry like the White Stag and the serpents adorned with their little crowns. Oh, these poets, always talking about things that don't really exist. And yet, maybe it's just because of this that their works are so lovely. But, my dear Janis, have you ever seen a nymph with sorrowing eyes right here in the sea, in our very own sea? Nymphs have such sorrowful eyes because they have to swim in the water all alone, without ever sharing the love of a man.'

"I didn't know what to reply and so Thymiane continued:

" 'If you want me to, I'll show you a nymph but one whose eyes are not sad at all. Right away, tonight. The moonlight is just right for it. And, as you know, I have magic powers all my own.'

" 'That you are a sorceress is true enough. All right, show me what you can do.'

"I sat down on a sand dune and stared out into the darkened sea across which the moon had cast a long silvery thread of light.

" 'Close your eyes,' she commanded, suddenly addressing me with the familiar 'thou.' 'Count up to thirteen three times and when you then open your eyes you'll see a living nymph. However, if you open them before then, you're lost and all of your poems will instantly dissolve into water. You only have but to believe what I tell you.'

" 'I've known for a long time that you were a sorceress, a mysterious blend of bird and flower, of woman and—'

" 'Oh, stop composing poems and close your eyes now, and start counting.'

"I obeyed. 'One, two, three, four, five—'

" 'For the love of God now, remember you can't open your eyes!'

" 'Six, seven, eight, nine, ten, eleven, twelve, thirteen.'

"I heard the rustling of a woman's dress and in the next moment the splashing of water. I counted a second time and then a third. I heard her call out with laughter in her voice and opened my eyes. She was swimming far out in the sea, her body shimmering palely against the dark water. She raised her arm in greeting and beckoned me to come to her. I stood there as though turned to stone. Even today I still can't understand why I didn't plunge into the water in order to overtake her. But that's my cursed nature, I guess, I never leap into cold water—I hesitate at the decisive moment. Just like a little boy I obeyed her command to continue walking and to wait for her behind a nearby willow bush while she got dressed again. To look behind me though, that she couldn't forbid me. Indeed, she had not lied to me, she actually was a nymph. On the following day I saw her again, this time at the opera where a famous Russian tenor was going to sing. She was wearing dark glasses and had on a black satin gown with long sleeves and a daring dècolletage and a sash of a sea green hue. Her neck seemed so white and she wore no jewelry at all. She talked only about the concert and acted as if absolutely nothing had happened the evening before. I escorted her home, but then, as we reached the door of her villa, she suddenly left me almost without saying a word. She closed the door so quickly and locked it behind her so rapidly that you might have thought she were fleeing from some thief. In the stillness of the brightly moonlit evening I wandered back along the same path on the shore and there in the moist sandy beach I saw the imprint of her naked feet. I bent down—"

Excitedly Ruth suddenly interrupted him, "Oh, now I understand—that's what it's all about, I mean your poem 'The Delicate Footprint.' I read it in the newspaper. At that time, of course, I didn't know to whom it was dedicated. I was moved by it and I learned it by heart." Janis continued:

"I really can't judge how great her talent was as a harpist. The critics praised her as a distinguished artist, and still her public appearance was always very modest. My mother, who had painted her portrait, said that she looked like the angel depicted by Melozzo da Forli in the Vatican Palace. She always wore her hair in a somewhat madonnalike fashion with her ears always covered. But still, her long hair was always luxuriantly curled and seemed to frame her face. A picture postcard of the Melozzo angel, the one playing a viola da gamba, used to hang above my bed. Even in the portrait my mother painted Thymiane is gazing upward toward heaven but with such earthly eyes!"

Janis stopped speaking as if he needed some time in order to free himself from the images he had summoned forth. After a moment Ruth said:

"You dedicated your first volume of poems to her, but why? She hardly understood our language."

"Oh, but she was so musically gifted that she could recite my poems by heart after I had read them to her only a few times—without understanding any of the words. It was only while listening to her reciting my verses that I became aware of what my words were saying and what I hadn't said. She had a very supple voice in which it seemed as if all the songs of the birds in the forests and all the waves of the sea would resound. Did she ever return from Siberia, I wonder? Is she now in Berlin again? In my letters I asked you repeatedly about her whereabouts but you never answered any of my questions about her. Tell me, Ruth, did she return?"

"Yes, this year. It would have been better though if she hadn't come back at all."

"How can you say such a thing!"

Looking Janis straight in his eyes, Ruth replied in a completely toneless voice, "While in Siberia her nose was frozen off, her whole nose." She was silent for a moment and Janis, too, said nothing. After a while she continued, "Now she doesn't have any nose at all. They sewed a glob of flesh on her face but she still looks awful, just like a turkey."

"Oh God, how awful! My poor Thymiane—I can't imagine it—such a beautiful woman—But then, after all, what does a nose really matter anyway? A man doesn't think with it and you don't need one to play a harp or to recite poems or to fathom the soul of a creative spirit. We don't need it

either to write or to read and we can still embrace the beauty
of nature, the glory of a sunflower, even without a nose."

While speaking Janis had become so excited that his voice
began to stutter and crack as though he were trying to convince himself of the truth of what he was saying. Without
paying any attention to him, Ruth continued:

"No one can stand even to look at her face now; her head,
everything about her seems disfigured. The very sight of her
is disgusting."

"I don't believe it! Thymiane's charm can't be created or
lost by just her nose. I could still love her today just as much
as I did on that moonlit night. A nose! My God, a nose
doesn't have anything at all to do with what a person really
is inside him."

"If you had only seen her you wouldn't say that."

"Ruth, I never would have thought that you, you of all
people, would place such importance on external things.
The outward appearance of a person is just like a dress and
who could ever really love a dress? For a short time it looks
pretty and you can like it, but it's not something decisive in
our lives."

"You're only saying that because you haven't seen her yet.
Her looks aren't just a minor defect; she's disfigured, absolutely deformed."

"What's a physical deformity in comparison with true
inner beauty?" He buried his face in his hands, unable
to comprehend how much Thymiane must have suffered
already and how much she must be suffering even yet. "You
know, Ruth, imprisonment was far more difficult for artists,
I mean the world-famous artists who had played such an
extraordinary role in the world while their lives were still
free! They suffered a hundred times more than doctors or
teachers. I once shared the barracks with the world-renowned
Russian actress L—— in one of the filthiest transit camps in
Siberia. A few of her remarks about Stalin had sufficed to
have her deported to the Arctic Circle. In the same barracks
there was also another actress, and can you guess what they
did to wile away their free time? Both of them were too weak
and sickly to do any physical labor. Just imagine it, they
used to compare their lice, and then L—— would proudly

announce to everyone that her lice were fatter and larger than those of her colleague."

Night had fallen and a large moon stood out in the heavens, but the two didn't move from their places on the doorstep of the shack.

"Please, Ruth, tell me everything you know about Thymiane," Janis pleaded.

"Now, whenever anyone comes to visit her, she puts on a mask. All you can see though is her toothless mouth and her eyes—they're still very beautiful. It's really not a mask, it's only a black piece of cloth with three holes in it. She's afraid of scaring off the few who still come to visit her."

"Those repelled by her looks are unworthy even of being in her presence!"

"My dear Janis, those are just nice theories dreamed up in your loneliness. Imagining something is quite different from experiencing it."

"But how does she live?"

"She receives a very small pension from the government even though she is a German. Because of her marriage to her half brother she was granted Soviet Russian citizenship. Sometimes, too, her neighbors bring her little gifts. Her former colleagues, though, don't bother about her. Her old seamstress, as well as her maid and butler, bring her things now and again whenever they receive a package from America."

"And how is she taking all this?"

"I don't know. She hardly speaks anymore. In any case, the things that people bring her she doesn't eat by herself; she shares them with her animals."

"Animals? Does she work in a zoo?"

"She has a little menagerie right in her own room—a turtle and two parakeets. The birds are so used to her now that they even peck the food right out of her mouth. She bills and coos with them, and when she does her voice becomes very soft and tender. As soon as the birds begin to flutter around her she doesn't seem distorted anymore. She has some guinea pigs too—no, they're not guinea pigs really, they're hamsters, golden hamsters. They run around her room like little puppies. Whenever someone gives her some lettuce—something really special even for us—she always feeds it to the hamsters. She sits on the floor and plays with them just like a little child. In her yard she once found a blackbird with a broken wing and she set it so skillfully that even a very talented veterinarian couldn't have done it any better.

"Once when I stopped by to see her, she said: 'I'm so happy today!' 'Why?' I asked. 'Just imagine it, my blackbird flew away this morning, yes, it was able to fly again! How happy that makes me! It was really a wonderful sight. At first it fluttered somewhat uncertainly and then, all of a sudden, it was as if it were intoxicated with its ability to fly once more. It flew up into the nearest tree and began to sing. It was thanking me with its song; I know it was. Animals are far more appreciative and faithful than people.' "

"And isn't there anyone who can mend Thymiane's broken wings? Ruth, tell me everything, everything you know. Don't conceal a thing."

"She chatters with her animals and imitates the voices of her birds. Really, it's almost eerie. But the stench in her room—"

"Oh, if I could only speak to her again, just once more to hear her soft melodious voice!"

"I've already told you, Janis, her voice has become hoarse and difficult to understand. You wouldn't recognize it."

"A person always remains what he really is deep down inside him, even after being banished to Siberia, even after death itself."

"What it's like after death, I don't know, but anyone who has returned from Siberia is a different person. You ought to know. Everyone changes from day to day; we, too, have changed."

It was almost with the sense of physical pain that Ruth suddenly realized that the man who was sitting next to her on the doorstep of his forest shack was a wholly different person from the man with whom she had lived together in dreams for fifteen long years and for whose sake she had traveled some six thousand kilometers.

(Randolph J. Klawiter)

To Zenta Maurina, every being has its reason for existence and an inevitable responsibility. A writer's task is "to humanize the dehumanized world."[11] Thus she valiantly defends the good, the beautiful, and the suffering. The works of Zenta Mauriņa serve as an uncompromising manifestation of intellectual power and humanity. The writer's *credo* is expressed in her own words: "In compassion, the soul of our neighbor opens for us like a bud in the sun. Pain is a bond of all the living. *Amo ergo sum.*"[12] Zenta Mauriņa's works have been published in many languages; in German alone she has about twenty volumes. Some of them have gone through more than half a dozen editions. In 1968, the government of the Federal Republic of Germany awarded Zenta Mauriņa the Order of Merit of the first class.

The greatest contemporary Latvian playwright is Mārtiņš Zīverts (b. 1903; now living in Stockholm). After studying philosophy, he turned to writing and has contributed over forty dramas which excel in stagecraft and strict technique. At the beginning of his comedy *The Chinese Vase* (1940), Zīverts symbolically refers to a dragon whose image is later reflected on a vase and begins to dominate the plot. Since that moment, symbolism is discernible in the majority of his works. The dramatist favors unpretentious strivers and scoffs at conceited and ostentatious notables and usurpers, as in *The One Who Doesn't Exist* (1948), *The Jester* (1953), and *Man Wants to Live* (1966).

Classicism was revived in the first anthologies of Jānis Medenis (b. 1903; in 1947 deported to Siberia; died in Latvia, 1961): *Towers at the Horizon* (1926), *Whetstone* (1933), *The Might* (1936), and *The Eternal Day* (1937). His favorite themes were nature, eroticism, and irrational nationalism. Medenis invented original combinations of encomiastic verses, based upon folklore.

Vilis Lācis (1904–1966) novelized the lives of sailors in the trilogy *Birds Without Wings* (1931–1933). He developed a close relationship with the Latvian Ministry of Social Affairs, which, in 1934, filmed his reportorial novel *The Fisherman's Son*

---

[11] Zenta Maurina, *Die Aufgabe des Dichters in unserer Zeit* (Munich, 1965), p. 167.

[12] Zenta Maurina, *Sirds Mozaika* (Göteborg, 1947), p. 39.

(1933). This was followed by *People in Masks* (1935), *The Stony Road* (1937–1938), and *The Edge of the Marsh* (1940). When the Soviet troops invaded Latvia in 1940, Vishinsky appointed Lācis the Minister of Internal Affairs. Only then was it disclosed that he had been a communist since 1928. In 1944, Lācis became a puppet premier of occupied Latvia. To please the regime, he rewrote his books and carried out mass executions and deportations. The Soviet government granted him the Stalin Award, but his readers and national communists branded him a traitor. He also published the novels *The Village on the Coast* (1953) and *After the Storm* (1962).

A score of volumes has been written by Jānis Širmanis (b. 1904; now in St. Mary's, Ohio). His tetralogy of fairy tales, *Kriksis* (1947–1955), illustrates the adventures of the vivacious dog Kriksis. This book, as well as *Evening Guests* (1961) and *The World of Wonders* (1966), can be found in almost every Latvian home. Anthropomorphism, *savoir faire,* and sophism are Širmanis' characteristics.

One of the most productive writers of prose is Anšlavs Eglītis (b. 1906; now in Pacific Palisades, Calif.). He stirred the public with the novel *The Hunters of Brides* (1940) in which caricatured, frivolous students carry out their projects with *animo et fide* and with macabre humor. In *Homo Novus* (1943), he novelized artists at work and in their love affairs. It was followed by the historical narrative *The Death of Genghis Khan* (1948) and the adventurous *Ajurjonga* (1955), a novel about Mongolia. Altogether, Eglītis wrote fourteen novels, twelve volumes of stories and tales, and eight plays. In his numerous works, placid and eloquent detailed descriptions prevail.

The novelist Antons Rupainis (b. 1906; now in Minneapolis), achieved recognition with his narrative of the Dominicans, entitled *The White Fathers* (1936–1937). The historical trilogy *Mary Awakes* (1951–1956) and the novel *The Salt of the Earth* (1955) prove Rupainis' thorough research and inexhaustible imagery. He uses strong subplots and interlards pleonasm with provincialisms.

Ģirts Salnais (b. 1906; now in St. Louis), has displayed his artistry in the novels *Ochre* (1943), *Tatters in the Wind* (1952), *Springs of Fire* (1955), *The Onion and the Orchid* (1965), and, more recently, *Slaves of the Heart* (1968), which is an anthology of twelve stories. In these, as well as in the four previous collections, Salnais treats contemporary issues with both gallantry and satire.

Konstantīns Raudive (b. 1909; now living in Germany) was inspired by Miguel de Unamuno, whom he came to know in Spain. In the trilogy *The Memoirs of Sylvester Pērkons* (1946–1948), the novels *The Damned Souls* (2 vols., 1948–1949), *The Invisible Light* (1954), *And Forgive Us Our Trespasses* (1959), *The Brightness and the Twilight* (1966), and the philosophical treatise *The Chaosman and His Subdual* (1951), the author deals with the existence of God and the meaning of the universe and man. Raudive studied philosophy and psychology in Paris, Edinburgh, and Uppsala, putting a special emphasis on posthumous phenomena. Having experimented in parapsychology for three years, in 1968 he wrote the controversial and sensational book *The Inaudible Becomes Audible*.

Knuts Lesiņš (b. 1909; now in Minneapolis), is a connoisseur of literature and music. His volume of stories *Omens in the Dark* (1938) and his novel *The Seal of Love* (1943) depict the work and the affairs of artists. Individuals of various milieux meet to create a climax in his collections *The Wine of Eternity* (1949), *Proud Hearts* (1952), and *Under the Foreign Stars* (1956). Lesiņš deals with psychological conflicts and is frequently derisive.

Sincere religious and patriotic meditations permeate the poetry of Marija Andžāne (b. 1906; living in Albany, N.Y.). The virtuosity of her crystalline lyrics is evident in the collections *The Morning* (1933) and *In the Gates of Anxiety* (1951). She has also written prose.

Velta Toma (b. 1912; now in Toronto, Canada) made her debut with the collection of poems *The Surmise* (1943), but her genuine talent triumphs in the long facile poem *Saturday in the Province Selonia* (1953), her sonnets: *The Eternal Game* (1960), and other books.

In the collections of poems *The Yellow-Hammer* (1939), *The Rainbow* (1940), and *Transience* (1942), Andrejs Eglītis (b. 1912; now in Stockholm) has left a unique imprint on the literature by treating contemporary issues in romantic triplets. When foreign troops devastated Latvia, Eglītis acquired *courage sans peur,* and it was during this time that he mastered technique. His typical run-on lines frequently shift to rhythmic staccato verse, achieving striking effects of sound and emotion. In the cantata *God, Thy Earth Is Aflame* (1943), which secured his fame, the poet addresses the national experience to God. Within the work he implements and expands upon the Lord's Prayer.

GOD, THY EARTH IS AFLAME— in fires of hatred and sin!
God, Thy earth is aflame—dark with sighs the heavens mourn!
The bird of ill omen laments for heroes forlorn.
    God, Thy earth is aflame!

Cities lie scattered in ruins, villages trodden down,
Deep into dust of destruction oak-trees must lower their
        crown.
    God, can this be the Judgment Day?
    In hatred
    Body and soul vanish away!

Raise up the cities from dust, the humbled oak-trees unbend,
To those overtaken by storms a glimmer of hopefulness lend.
    Grayheaded fathers, grayheaded mothers,
    Let us fervently pray to God,
    That the harsh winds that blew through your lifetime
    May now soften, may sink to rest.
        Do not waver, warrior band,
        Peace is still far from our native land.
    Let old eyes behold the sun
    Calmly when the day is done,
    And let young eyes sparkle bright
    To excelling morning light!
    Let black stumps give a thousandfold

Offshoots of the purest gold!
Grayheaded fathers, grayheaded mothers,
Let us fervently pray to God,
That He may give us a green road to the churchyard
And, for a pillow, our native earth.
    What do I care where I sleep,
    If over me Latvia's willows weep.

    God, Thy earth is aflame!

The deeps and the heights obey Thee—stay evil and gales
    with Thy call,
And make the wide world a table, a sacred table for all.
    God, pity us and show Thy grace,
    Turn not away
    From us Thy face!
    Wives and mothers that are young,
    Let a prayer be fervently sung:
    May the black wolves not find their prey:
    Keep them from our lambs away.
        Cradles keep rocking, rock without ceasing,
        Carry our Latvia on to new heights.
    Wives and mothers that are young,
    Let a prayer be fervently sung:
    May a cradle for our native land
    Be rocked by each tender hand.
    Keep him believing, save him with prayers,
    Child of hopes in a cradle of sighs;
    Heaven be a blessing, earth a caressing,
    Thy love through misfortune
    Radiate through

    God, Thy earth is aflame!

Do not allow the sun and the moon to be wrapped in red
    vapours,
Rule the nations to cherish and fear Thy name.
    A prayer is rising
    Upwards to Thee:

Latvia's sons desire to be free!
Oh, my land, land of my fathers!
God, oh God, come to our aid,
To protect our sacred borders;
Enemies rise from east and west.
Oh, my land, land of my fathers!
How to keep thee, how protect?
Shower, God, Thy golden arrows,
Evil-willing foes arrest!
Let the eyes of men be bright
And their souls together alight,
Oh, send a sign through our night.
Danger threatens cradles and graves! Danger!
Let not hate the nations perturb,
Heavy steps our cornfields disturb;
Bless us and teach us then
Like brothers to live, to die like men.
And once a nation is born,
Apart do not let it be torn!
Let not a nation's heart
Be torn apart!

God, Thy earth is aflame!

Hand us a shield of faith bright over valleys of death
That we through changing times may feel the eternal breath.
Accept the prayer of sorrow;
Love!
Sow love in the hearts of tomorrow.
Sons of our sacred native land,
Sacred company of our maids
Pray, oh, fervently pray!
We are new bells—Thou art our ringing,
Let us sing Thy name joyfully,
Let over childhood and our tender birches
Thy golden splendour lie increasingly.
We are new bells—Thou art our ringing.
Descend on us, be in us, sacred flame.

To help us wear the pure white crown,
    As did our mothers,
To help us wield white honour's sword,
    As did our fathers.
We are a small nation—God is our fire,
Let sacred longing make us pure,
To be new bells, Oh, Lord, and ringing sure!
We are fresh springs—Thou art the living water.
    May changing weather leave us clear,
    Passing by, however near!
We are the hope and blossom of our native land!
    If heaven and stone should scream,
    And earth should quiver and burst,
    And darkness hide no beam,
    I would still worship my God.
        Our Father who art in heaven,
        Hallowed be Thy Name.
He will not forget a small nation
And He alone will know the day,
When having banished darkness
He will lead us a sunlit way.
        Thy kingdom come,
        Thy will be done,
        On earth as it is in heaven.
Oh, does the star of peace still hide,
No lightness weary warriors guide?
Oh, Latvian nation, you must raise
Your suffering, turning it to praise.
        Give us this day our daily bread,
        And forgive us our trespasses,
        As we forgive those
        Who trespass against us.
Our eyes in prayer look to heaven;
Beneath us all has shrunk to dust;
But in His mercy, He shall purge us,
Our God, in whom we trust.
        And lead us not into temptation,

But deliver us from evil.
For Thine is the kingdom, the power and the
    glory . . .
Through dust and centuries,
Through ages, lost and vain,
God will allow our flag
To remain.
The day is near—we dedicated to our land,
Let us be a sea of rising hopes;
The hour is near—from a lowly sand
Let us reach mountainlike
To a new day,
Towards God!
From new earth to new heaven!
For ever and ever. Amen!

(Velta Snikere)

"In our burning churches we desperately appealed to God," the poet wrote. Music for the cantata was composed by Lūcija Garūta, Tālivaldis Ķeniņš, and Brūno Skulte. Since then, Eglītis has devoted his life solely to the betterment of humanity and the defense of freedom. In the volume *On the Shield* (1947) he stated, "I have neither a life nor a death of my own, only that of my nation." The use of prophetic utterance infused with imagery is continued in *The Fiery Words* (1949), *Otranto* (1956), and *I Love, Love* (1962).

After her graduation in Romance philology and the study of prosody, Veronika Strēlerte (b. 1912; residing in Stockholm) became the most refined Latvian lyricist. She employs a carefully selected vocabulary; her expression is sparsely worded and musical. Every stanza reveals the noble intellect of the poetess. In the foreground of the volumes *Simple Words* (1937), *The Rain Drop* (1940), *The Moon River* (1945), *Silver Waters* (1949), *Deserts of Light* (1951), *The Servant of Armour* (1953), and *Years of Mercy* (1961), stands the sun—the Latvian symbol of wisdom and purity—and water, which signifies the perpetual rhythm of the universe. Some of Veronika Strēlerte's poems deal with patriotic emotions and evoke nostalgia, as in "Places":

> Some places on earth will continue living within me
> As long as I live,
> Unchanged by all change,
> Untouched by vicissitudes,
> Sheltered as under an angel's wing.
> Streets broken up, and houses razed to the ground,
> The unrecognizable face of cities
> Twisted into grimace—
> But I shall find the houses I know, the familiar
> Corners of streets, my forever scent-laden gardens,
> And fields in shadowy twilight
> With dark golden slumbering stacks of rye.
>
> (Ruth Speirs)

Jānis Klīdzējs (b. 1914; now living in Napa, Calif.) made his debut with the novel *The Youths* (1942), which reached a total of five editions. Tranquil and serene descriptions of cheerful events interchange with abrupt statements to achieve dramatic vividness. The style is lyrical throughout and, there-fore, critics recommended that he devote more effort to poetry. Klīdzējs endowed his hero Andris Rugājs with altruism and tremendous vigor:

> He scudded along. Caught the train. Jumped in. Then he stood in the door clutching in his hand the red roses he had received upon his departure. Still he felt Susy's arms around his shoulders. The wind tangled his hair and blew it into his eyes. Andris tossed his head and gazed into the dark summer night. The train sped on.
> Stations. Strange people. Stations again.
> Bright shooting stars dashed across the sky of his native land.
> Mary, Peter, Susy . . . , he contemplated. Perhaps those are sparkles of your souls in the great soul of God. You still hesi-tate to be greedy, brazen-faced, and rude and, therefore, you are orphans in this cruel world.

In the distance horses neighed, dogs barked, and someone was singing. He could hear it above the clanking of the train.

Suddenly Andris felt a burden upon himself, as if he had to bear the weight of the mountains he was passing. "My God, what should I do?" he whispered, but was too inexperienced to perceive an answer. "There is a great conflagration in my bosom, and I want to recast many a thing."

(Aleksis Rubulis)

In the postwar period, Klīdzējs produced several volumes of short stories, beginning with *The River Flows* (1945). The next, *Lovers and Haters* (1946), contains eleven outstanding stories, among them "The Man with a Stone Heart." Its protagonist, Dunda, displays polarly opposite characteristics: the good and the evil combat each other. "Dunda has the heart of a human and of a wolf," the writer explains. The considerate girl Marita thinks that the man is not evil; he is only miserable because he lives in an ignorant society. "No one has ever loved Dunda, not even in his childhood." The world has shown Dunda only its wolf's heart and, therefore, has received his impervious rejection in return: "I don't need your love!" The collections *People on the Bridge* (1948), *The Shelter* (1948), *The Shared Sin* (1951), and *The Horizon* (1968) display a variety of topics and styles. In *The Horizon,* the story "The Brother's Return" tragically portrays Stanislavs' homecoming from Siberia and the immediate sacrifice of his life:

Augusts, startled, heard the sound of a footfall. He glanced at weapons on the wall, then at Lūcija and Stanislavs. Lūcija turned pale and dropped the slices of bread she held. In an instant someone pounded on the door and shouted in a hollow voice, "Open! Silāns, give yourself up voluntarily! If you don't, we will hurl hand grenades in!"

Augusts was confused. He seized his rifle immediately.

"Oh, Jesus!" Lūcija exclaimed desperately.

Stanislavs noticed the eyes of his brother and his brother's wife filled with horror. At that very moment he recalled substitutional incidents among his former comrades-in-arms during the siege, and he announced, "I must go! Augusts has to remain! They will not recognize me at night! He has to hide."

Stanislavs made an imperious gesture toward his brother and uttered through clenched teeth, "Take care of yourself. I shall go."

Then he rushed to the door and said, "I am coming. Just let me put some clothes on."

He took Augusts' wet coat and hat, then whispered to his brother, "Be calm! You must live! You have a wife and children—Lūcija, hold him!"

He hugged both Augusts and Lūcija, then pushed them into another room.

"I shall escape if possible—Meanwhile, you must move out—May God protect you!"

Stanislavs' face twitched as he looked at them for the last time.

"Don't do anything foolish," he warned his brother, and with an unfaltering step approached the door and opened it.

"Hands up!" several voices resounded.

"Did you leave your lair for the sake of kids?"

"Where are your weapons?"

"In the woods," Stanislavs replied.

"That suits us fine. We will get all of you."

The beam of a flashlight illuminated the face of Stanislavs.

"You are lean as a wolf," one of them grinned.

The other slapped his face.

"Let's search the house," a Russian yelled in a shrill voice.

"There is no need," another injected. "We got him. I can't bear the screaming of women and children every night. Let's go! Move!"

The footsteps of the group resounded over the courtyard.

Flattening himself against the wall, Augusts had heard everything, including the slap on his brother's face.

"They are taking him—taking him away," he murmured.

Lūcija collapsed on a bed. Only now she burst into tears.

Augusts started to recover his consciousness. What had happened? They seized my brother for an execution? But I am still safe? What did Stanislavs say as if in a nightmare? He volunteered to die instead of me? They are kidnapping my own brother, but I am protecting my skin by playing a coward! He grabbed the rifle and attached some hand grenades to his belt.

"Darling—dear Augusts!" Lūcija attempted to hold him. "Don't go, don't—Stanislavs said you should save the children—think of me—You can't—"

"Let me go!" he fumed. "Let go! I will kick all of them into the beyond like turnips! I am telling you—They are going to murder my brother, but you—Have you lost your mind?"

"No! It will not do any good. Stanislavs said—" Lūcija tried to stop him.

Augusts broke her grip and drew her aside.

"Do you realize that within an hour they will be after us? They will recognize Stanislavs. I am going to free him! And you, you wake up the children immediately and leave the house—Let one of the neighbors take you to another parish—to our relatives—perhaps friends—or strangers—Just don't remain here. Save our children and yourself—God be with you—"

(Aleksis Rubulis)

Among the eight stories in the volume *They* (1954), "The Minister of the Foreign Affairs Is Ill" excels. In it, Sir Mitchell Silverheap destroys many countries with a single stroke of his red pencil. This treatise reflects the resentment and disappointment of millions of Europeans regarding the consent of Franklin Roosevelt and Winston Churchill to keep the Soviet military forces in Eastern Europe in order to please Joseph Stalin. In the novels *Janitor* (1955), *The Blue Mountains* (1960), *The Snows* (1963), and *Life, Dear Life* (1967) Jānis Klīdzējs focused on human nature in contemporary society and treated it with candid sincerity, humor, and satire. The novel *The Child of Man* (1956) is Klīdzējs' *chef-d'oeuvre,* in which the boy, Bons, is a unique and most enthralling prototype in world literature. Jānis Klīdzējs studied at the University of Latvia, and earned his master's degree in psychology at the University of California at Berkeley. Bons has benefited considerably from Klīdzējs' psychological studies. "His fingers itch ceaselessly to do something"; he is active, naive, and convincingly natural in his pranks and secrets.

Vilis Cedriņš (b. 1914; died in Siberia, 1946, of scurvy) devised new Latvian meters in the volumes of ballads and poems *The Silver Horseman* (1935) and *The North Orchards* (1942). Cedriņš portrayed the picturesque countryside of Latvia and national growth in a virile and hymnic style.

Psychological conflicts and the egocentricity of displaced persons are recorded by Kārlis Ķezbers (b. 1914; now in Chicago), in the novel *The Duchy of Main* (1960). His essential contribution, however, lies in two additional novels and the short story collections *The Mosaic of Riga* (1961) and *Servants of Dr. Applebee* (1965). Kārlis Ķezbers excels in juvenile literature permeated with picturesque glimpses and restrained emotions.

In addition to prose, Ingrida Vīksna (I. Fogele, b. 1920; now in Toronto, Canada) has manifested her talent in the volumes of poetry *The Bitter Joy* (1943), *I Express My Gratitude* (1955), and *My Walk Doesn't Cease* (1968). Vīksna's poetry exhibits her singularity.

Velta Snikere (b. 1920; living in London), exhibited new forms in the collections *Surmise Unceasing* (1961) and *The Call* (1967). The Hindu mysticism present in her work is due to her study of yoga, which she is teaching in London, and to her dancing of *bharata natya* and *kathak* on the stages of Ceylon in 1955–1956. The poet's adherence to Rilke has resulted in her use of suffix formations. Now and then, she is both introspective and playful, "I am a deceased trouble and an unborn joy." Velta Snikere considers herself an outsider, a poet who does not belong to any school or ism, while critics brand her works as surrealistic:

Lapis

Light poured out, to be grasped in light,
Sap of life, pulsating;
To obtain shape
Sunk into silence:
Amber.

Vanquish in Love

Vanquish in love,
Long enough have you been trying to harm me.
Send your doves upon my shoulders and arms—
I will not startle them by turning sharply.
Let your flowers arise from my open palms—
Your butterflies will not alarm me,
Nor your nightingales.

(Translated by the author)

Valentine Hermane-Daly (b. 1924; resides in Elgin, Ill.) adheres strictly to traditional forms in the poems of *The Quest* (1959), but in her next collection, *Not All Vanishes* (1963), she displays her natural exuberance for wholesome fancy and controlled emotions in free verse. The stories contained in *On the Brink of Shadows* (1965) employ surprise endings reminiscent of O. Henry. Her expression is gentle; rarely does it reveal the subtle irony found in "The Precaution" (1968):

I recall
a man
who in his dream
stepped
on a sliver of glass.
Oh my,
what aches and pains
he claimed!
Aroused,
he put his boots on.
And since,
even in sleep,
he never takes them off.

(Aleksis Rubulis)

The poetry of Andris Vējāns (b. 1927; active in occupied Latvia) falls into two categories: first, passionate and ornate stanzas about his native countryside, revealing a true poet's gift and, secondly, worthless political products imposed by socialist realism. The ranting nature of many of Vējāns' verses are indicative of either immaturity or ruthlessness. In the poem "Give Me the Anger of the Thunder," he craves for vengeance. An element of force may be found even in the poem entitled "Love":

> Where to find a word, strong and warm,
> That expresses beauty and power
> With the thunder of a storm
> And with the tremble of a flower?
>
> Could the thunder give a clue?
> —My heart was struck by your love
> As by a bolt from the blue.
>
> (Aleksis Rubulis)

Vējāns published the collections *The Youth* (1953), *The Sun Rises* (1957), *Gulls Call One Another* (1959), and *Mountain Eyes* (1965).

A great number of other writers and poets are scattered throughout the world. Among the most talented of these are Dzintars Freimanis, Ilze Šķipsna, Valdis Krāslavietis, Eduards Freimanis, Indra Gubiņa, Alberts Spoģis, Rita Gāle, Eduards Silkalns, and Aivars Ruņģis.

Lithuanian Literature

Folklore

After the extinction of Old Prussian and Curonian languages, only Lithuanian and Latvian remained in the Baltic group. Because of their ancient and close linguistic relationship, the two nations have folklore similar in its content and form. As a matter of fact, Lithuanians have thirty-seven old folk songs in common with Latvians, which lets us assume that they originated during the period when all the Balts formed one nation. Lithuanian, among the oldest of Indo-European languages, is rooted directly in Sanskrit and, therefore, is used in comparative linguistics. Perhaps this is why Lithuanian folklore has some characteristics identical with that of the Orient, as shown, for example, in "Frogs, the Sun, and God":

> Once a frog heard gossip that the Sun had decided to get married. She summoned other frogs and announced, "Do you realize that bad times will befall us? The Sun already makes brooks and swamps dry in summer; but when she[1] becomes a mother and has to worry about the warmth of her children, we'll find water nowhere, not even in rivers and ponds. We must go to God and complain!"
>
> Having reached this important decision, the frogs croaked loudly while they leaped to the dear God to lodge a complaint. However, God wasn't home.
>
> When the Sun found out that the frogs wanted to accuse her, she became angry and said, "I am warming the whole world and will do it forever; but from now on I exclude this vermin."
>
> The frogs admitted their guilt and started to shun the Sun. Even now frogs leap out of their hiding places and croak only after sunset or when it is cloudy. They are always cold.
>
> (Aleksis Rubulis)

[1] In Lithuanian and Latvian the sun is of feminine gender and it can be replaced with a personal pronoun, as is the case with any other noun. The moon, on the other hand, belongs to the masculine gender. Therefore, many myths in the folklore of both nations speak of the marriage of the moon and the sun.

The sun was considered a deity by all Indo-European tribes during the Bronze Age (2000–900 B.C.). In Lithuanian mythology this cult survived longer, because the ancient Lithuanians lived in an isolated area scarcely affected by the old Greek and Roman cultures. Literacy was introduced only toward the end of the Middle Ages, and the absence of it promoted the creation and preservation of oral literature.

The Archives of the Lithuanian Academy of Sciences has collected approximately 195,000 folk songs, i.e., *dainos*, with about 30,000 melodies. The *daina* reflects the work, joy, struggle, nature, and even historical vestiges of the nation. Despite the wisdom and richness of wit found in the *dainos,* the style is unusually simple, refined, and elegant. This encouraged Chopin, Schumann, Schubert, and many others to compose from them. These songs were translated by Johann G. Herder, Adalbert von Chamisso, and Richard Dehmel. Their charm excited Gotthold E. Lessing, and Wolfgang Goethe included some of them in his play *The Fisheress* (1782).

Neither Lithuanian nor Latvian folk songs can be translated into any foreign language without drastically reducing their value in form and content. The Baltic languages have highly inflected verb forms and, therefore, it is often possible to omit personal pronouns; there are no articles, but innumerable diminutives exist which usually express endearment. Many of the Lithuanian folk songs have been translated into English, German, Finnish, Russian, Czech, Estonian, French, and Polish.

The Moon Wedded the Sun

The moon wedded the sun
in the first springtime.

The sun rose in the dawn,
the moon abandoned her,

wandered alone, afar,
and loved the morning star.

Angered, Perkunas[2] thundered
and cleft him with a sword:

[2] The mythological god of thunder and lightning.

—How could you dare to love
the daystar, drift away
in the night alone, and stray?

(Clark Mills)

Far Along the Meadow

Far along the meadow
Little birches grow;
There are three atossing, toss-toss, tossing,
Whispering together so:

—If I were a young man,
A ploughman on the hill,
All the sorrow, sorrow, oh, the whole world's sorrow,
With a ploughshare I would till.

If I were a young man,
A mounted gallant lord,
All the darkness, darkness, oh, the whole world's darkness,
I would lighten with my sword.

Far along the meadow
Little lindens grow;
There are three atossing, toss-toss, tossing,
Whispering together so:

—If I were a maiden,
My mother I would leave;
Of the sorrow, sorrow, oh, the whole world's sorrow,
Finest linens I would weave.

(Demie Jonaitis)

O Mother, My Heart and Life

O Mother, my heart and life,
Tell me the meaning of my dreams.
A jackdaw flew over the cherry orchard
Spinning green silk
And scattering white pearls.

O Son, my heart and life,
I will tell you the meaning of your dreams.
The jackdaw is your bride,
The green silk is her hair,
And the white pearls are tears.

(Robert Payne)

 Early Writings

Lithuanian literature was indirectly promoted by religious rivalry. Reformers discovered a fertile soil and moved in to spread their ideology. Thus, the first extant book published in the Lithuanian language is *Simple Words of the Catechism* (1547), translated by the Protestant pastor Martynas Mažvydas and printed in Königsberg. In 1549 he also published a collection of church songs. In 1590 another pastor, Jonas Bretkunas (1535–1602), translated the Bible, which remained in manuscript form at the library of Königsberg University. Danielius Kleinas (1609–1666), pastor of Tilsit, compiled the *Grammatica Lituanica* in 1653.

Bishop Merkelis Giedraitis realized that the Catholic Church had neglected its responsibility in Lituania and, therefore, many more of its members could be converted to Lutheranism and Calvinism. To remedy the situation he invited Jesuits to Lithuania. As a result, the Catholic Academy in Vilnius (1578) and several lower schools, as well as a printing press, were founded. Mikalojus Daukša (1527–1613), canon of Žemaičiai, translated the *Catechism* (1595). A Jesuit and professor at the Catholic Academy, Konstantines Sirvydas (1580–1631), compiled the *Dictionarium Trium Linguarum* (1629) and translated from the Polish the collection of sermons *Punktai Sakymu* (Vol. I, 1629; Vol. II, 1644). All of the aforesaid Catholic publications were manufactured in Vilnius. *Die Fabuln Aesopi zum Versuch nach dem Principio Lithuanicae linguae* (1706), a translation by Jonas Šulcas (1684–1710) of ten of Aesop's fables, was the first secular book in Lithuanian literature.

Kristijonas Donelaitis (1714–1780) was the first important Lithuanian poet. He was born into a Protestant farmer's family, studied at Königsberg University and, from 1743, was a pastor of Tolminkiemis. The university required that all theology majors be fluent in Latin. The New Testament was presented in Greek, but the Old Testament was explained in Hebrew. In addition, he was proficient in German and French and attempted to versify in foreign languages. Apparently, it was Donelaitis' thorough knowledge of Western and classical literature and his affection for it which led him to choose hexameter with a fair syllabotonic verse-structure for his epic poem *The Seasons* (written 1765–1775; first published 1818). However, the poet rejected the exaggerated idealization of rural life in the didactic works of Hesiod and Vergil. He also found James Thomson's sentimental emotions in *The Seasons* (1730) unfit for his epic. Donelaitis presented a realistic portrayal, true to the existing conditions of struggling serfs. Obviously, there is a sharp contrast between *The Seasons* and Greek and Roman heroic epics in regard to plot and eloquence. In the treatment, however, Goethe compared Donelaitis with Homer.[3]

Donelaitis' *The Seasons* is composed of four chapters: "Joys of Spring," "Summer Toils," "Autumn Wealth," and "Winter Cares." Thomson was the first modern poet to choose nature for his theme. Donelaitis also described natural scenery, animals and birds, but only as auxiliary to his exposition of man's environment, as in "Joys of Spring":

> The rats and skunks came forth from secret holes and nooks;
> Crows, ravens, magpies, owls sailed on from bough to bough.
> Mice, moldwarps and their young acclaimed the glowing warmth.
> The countless flies and bugs, mosquitos, gnats and fleas,
> In ever growing swarms were rallying each day
> And gaping all around to sting the rich and poor.
> The queen bee, too, called forth her subjects to the task,

[3] See Aleksis Rannit's "Kristijonas Donelaitis and Lithuanian Poetry," *Baltic Review*, no. 30 (Dec. 1965), pp. 48–64.

Commanding them to start again upon their work.
Soon endless swarms of them began to buzz and zoom,
Afifing merry tunes and flying far and wide;
Secluded in the nooks, lean spiders spun their threads,
Or, scaling up and down, stretched long entrapping nets.
Even the wolves and bears at the green forest's edge
Hunted in joyous mood for some unwary game.
It was a wondrous thing, that in the endless flock
Of warblers that came here, there was no bird that wept.

(Nadas Rastenis)

To Thomson, a prolonged eulogy of nature could become
tedious. Induced by the example of Alexander Pope, he interspersed his poem with tales, anecdotes, and lessons in physics
and geography. His work lacks unity; it reminds one of a collection of various poems. Donelaitis, on the other hand, fused his
epic by choosing the Lithuanian nation for his hero. Instead
of anecdotes obviously inserted to entertain, he incorporated
the dialogues of peasants in their joy, sorrow, and labor, as in
"Summer Toils":

As Krizas so complained, large crowds of men appeared,
Ashouting, "Jump, mow, rake, make hay and store away!"
The fields, like anthills, now began to swarm and buzz;
The farmers and the help swung scythes and shook their feet.
Indeed, it seemed as if an army set for war,
With shining metal blades, attacked the verdant meads.

(Nadas Rastenis)

The characters possess basic individuality; however, their
primary role is to supplement one another within the nation
as a whole, which they represent. To avoid monotony in pre-
senting everyday routine, Donelaitis varied his expression in
accord with the events, at times applying dynamic techniques.
While in the idylls of Johann H. Voss the happiness of country
people at their work is based upon their vitality and romance,
the heroes of *The Seasons* strive for security, as in "Autumn's
Wealth":

The wealth that the green meads displayed in merry **May**,
The gifts that the lush fields gave forth in joyous **June**,
We now have gathered and stored up beneath the roof;
These riches now we cook and eat each blessed day.
You there, you gaggling geese, and you too, quacking ducks,
Run—run and swim before the streaming rivers freeze.
You roosters and you hens, leave your dirt-pile a while;
Run once again and play before the snowdrifts come;
And think not that we keep and feed you in our barns
Because your clucks are sweet or your cackles are grand.
Ah no! It is because we like your tender meat.

(Nadas Rastenis)

Being a clergyman, Donelaitis inserted paternal reprimands and instructions. He witnessed the penetration of Western vices together with culture into Lithuania. Some of the didactic verses in *The Seasons* were paraphrased from the sermons he preached:

In olden days our folk had no books and no schools;
They were not taught their ABC's nor catechism.
They learned the Holy Script and Rule Divine by heart,
Yet they obeyed and praised God oft and more than we,
And went to church more faithfully on holy days.
But nowadays, good God, it is a shame to see,
How our Lithuanian folk, drest up in French attire,
Just now and then drop in the church to show themselves,
Then hasten to an inn to drink, carouse, and dance.
Ere long many of them, well-filled with alcohol,
Begin their boorish jokes and rough, indecent tales,
Yea, with expressions never heard inside the church,
Twist words into grossness and gossip wantonly.

(Nadas Rastenis)

In his reproofs, the language of Donelaitis is more stern but still restrained. Rarely does he use harsh comparisons: "But— 'tis a shame to tell it—they, like loutish swine, Began their brazen tales and their indecent songs." It is typical in *The Seasons* to procure God's blessings, e.g., in "Winter Cares":

> And so now let us part, and with the help of God
> Let's hurry to repair our implements and tools;
> But without Thy aid, our Father who'rt in heav'n
> We cannot reap the wealth the summer tenders us . . .
> Therefore, O Father, take paternal care of us
> And all our needs, and when the summertime doth come,
> Aid us afield, when we again shall toil and sweat.

(Nadas Rastenis)

Another great poet of the time was Antanas Baranauskas (1834–1902), Catholic bishop of Seinai. He accepted romanticism, which had been reinforced by the works of Adam Mickiewicz (1799–1855). Actually, Baranauskas occupied himself with poetry only before he was ordained a priest. He recognized the charm of his native land while studying in St. Petersburg, Rome, Munich, and Louvain. In 1858 and 1859, during his summer vacations at home, Baranauskas created the unforgettable poem *The Forest of Anykščiai*.[4] For him, the forest did not exist for its beauty alone. Even though he painted many woodland scenes in the poem's nearly 350 verses, the forest has its practical value:

> Forest and peasant knew no discord,
> Grew up together, aged in accord.
> To the Lithuanian, caveman of yore,
> The forest gave a strong wooden door;
> And since he never would hew the wood,
> Till aged it fell, the dry trees still stood.
> And e'en the forest did its full share:
> Gave the Lithuanian its love and care —
> Fed him on meat, fruit, honey of bees,
> And slew his foemen with storm-torn trees;
> In danger gave a safe place to hide,
> In sorrow did peace and cheer provide;

---

[4] A town in Lithuania.

It daily brought him joy, food, and health,
And yearly blessed him with ample wealth.

Once came a lengthy famine, alas!
Moss bread was eaten, soup cooked of grass;
And on the people meagerly fed,
Alack, a plague fell, festered and spread.
The wood took pity, dewy tears shed,
And in compassion audibly said:
"Starve not, dear brethren, be not so lax:
Blest is the hand that fashioned the ax!"
At the beginning men, with eyes wet,
Hewed not much wood, and that with regret.
Then their sons cut the trees with a frown;
And then the grandsons sold loads in town.
Fetching some forty cartloads away,
Gladly they took a shilling a day.
Wood prices fell, the trade still went on—
And soon the ancient forest was gone.
Surely 'tis pity even to think,
Most of the wood was sold for a drink.

(Nadas Rastenis)

Baranauskas has shown the nation's dependence upon its natural resources. The poem is saturated with enthusiasm for creative labor.

 ## Romanticism and Symbolism

Education and national literature were the main stimuli for freedom which manifested itself in the uprising of 1831. As a result, Russian authorities closed the University of Vilnius. In 1863, Lithuanians and Poles jointly organized an insurrection to put an end to the foreign rule, but they also failed. So as not to lose the occupied countries, the tsarist government decided to Russianize them forcibly. Thus, in 1865, a decree was passed which prohibited the use of Latin characters. This ban continued for forty years and involved Latgale, the eastern province of Latvia, as well. Because Lithuanian and Latvian sounds cannot be expressed by the Cyrillic alphabet, the regime expected the quick disappearance of national consciousness and renascence. Lithuanian political and cultural leaders realized the danger. They printed books in East Prussia and smuggled them into Lithuania by the thousands regularly. In Tilsit, Jonas Basanavičius (1851–1927) founded the first Lithuanian newspaper, *Aušra* [The dawn] (1883–1886) which was transported secretly across the border and became an important instrument. Among its contributors was the poet and priest Maironis, the poets Andrius Vištelis (1837–1912), Petras Arminas (1853–1885), Jonas Mačys Kėkštas (1867–1902), and Vincas Kudirka (1858–1899).

Jonas Maironis-Mačiulis (1862–1932) served both as a romantic poet and a prophet. He studied in Kiev and St. Petersburg, became a professor in St. Petersburg and Vilnius, and was ordained a priest. He began writing lyrics, many of which are set to music. The collection *The Voices of Spring* (1895) promoted the national resurrection and glorified the Lithuanian countryside. It went through six editions during his lifetime. After prohibition of the national anthem, Maironis composed a prayer that resounded all over the country:

> Protect, O Almighty, our beautiful homeland,
> The soil where we labor, where our fathers rest.
> Thy fatherly mercy is boundless and lasting;
> Hear us, Thy own children, long ages oppressed.
> Forsake not our land, All-Highest, while the fury rages;
> For Thou art our Hope and Vision, now and through
>   the ages.

> (Nadas Rastenis)

Maironis also wrote ballads and satires. His greatest contribution is a historical drama (a triology in verse): *The Death of Kestutis*[5] (1921), *Vytautas with the Crusaders* (1930), and *King*

---

[5] A Lithuanian king (c. 1300–1382).

Vytautas the Great (1930). He also introduced a new rhythmic pattern, established poetic norms, and brought in other formal innovations.

The symbolist Vydūnas (Vilius Storasta, 1868–1953) was not directly involved in political affairs. He studied literature and philosophy in Germany, then became a teacher. In his plays *The Shadows of Ancestors* (1908), *The Eternal Flame* (1912), and *Bells of the Sea* (1914), he expresses his theosophical wisdom combined with ethology and mysticism. Some of his comedies are based upon the life of Lithuanian society. Of all Vydūnas' works, the tragedy *The World on Fire* (1928) was most enthusiastically accepted by the public. It depicts military activity in Lithuania during World War I.

Jurgis Baltrušaitis (1873–1944) studied history and philosophy in Moscow, and traveled widely throughout Europe and the United States. From 1921 to 1939 he was the Lithuanian ambassador in the USSR, but in 1939 he settled in Paris, where he died. Baltrušaitis began publishing poetry in 1899, joining the symbolists. His first volumes, *Earthly Steps* (1911) and *The Mountain Path* (1912), were published in Russian. Only in 1930 did he start to publish in Lithuanian.

Morning Song

Dawn, bright herald, proclaims the accession of Day
To the valleys still heavy with night,
And the clouds of sheer opal and ruby make way
For the regal arrival of Light.

And the skies and the plains lie wide open, unfurled
From the cope to the dew-covered base,
As though God were withdrawing the veils of the world
From His infinite marvel of space.

Sudden shudders now pass through the bay, as it flings
Waves that whiten and roar and assault,
And the crystal of silence falls shattered and rings
Its joy to the jubilant vault. . . .

(Ants Oras)

Baltrušaitis strove for the cultivation of technique. Since he read works in many foreign languages, his anthologies *The Garland of Tears* (1942) and *Poems* (1948) reflect elements of many philosophies as well as asceticism.

Faustas Kirša (b. 1891) also employed symbolism in the poems of *The Whirlwind* (1918) and *Echoes and Reechoes* (1921). From 1922 to 1925, Kirša studied literature and esthetics in Berlin and was attracted by the metaphysics of Max Scheler and Schopenhauer. His later highly imaginative books, *Hymns* (1934), *Prayers on the Rock* (1937), *Pilgrims* (1938), and *In the Far Distance* (1947) are complex religious and philosophical meditations. In the satirical collection *Ashes* (Vol. I, 1930; Vol. II, 1938), Kirša scoffs at human weaknessess.

 ## Literature in the Twentieth Century

At the turn of the century, two important literary figures emerged: Krēvē and Mykolaitis-Putinas. Vincas Krēvē (1882–1954) studied at many institutions. In 1898, at the age of sixteen, he enrolled in a theological seminary in Vilnius but left it in 1900 and took up private studies, obtaining a high school diploma in 1904. In the same year he registered at the University of Kiev to study philosophy and history. There he wrote his first story, "The Fog," which was published in the journal *The Rainbow* in 1913. Because the university was forced to close temporarily during the 1905 revolution, Krēvē matriculated at the University of Lvov to major in Indo-European philology. He earned his doctorate in 1908 and was awarded a gold medal for his dissertation, "The Home of Indo-Europeans." Krēvē then worked as a teacher and consul in Baku, Azerbaijan, where he wrote *Šarūnas* (1911), a drama portraying the adventurous deeds of the legendary and ruthless Lithuanian chieftain Šarūnas, whose name appears in the *dainos*. *The Legends of the Old Folks of Dainava* (1912) revives ancient incidents based on folklore. In 1921 he published two collections of short stories, *The Dusk* and *Under a Thatched Roof*.

Krėvė was appointed a professor of Slavic languages and literatures at the University of Kaunas in 1922. His next drama, *Skirgaila*[6] (1922), was written in Russian, and only in 1924 did he translate it into Lithuanian. The playwright realistically depicts political discord fused with the clash between Christian and heathen traditions. His well-knit structure, unbiased character portrayal, and vivid dialogues make *Skirgaila* an outstanding work. The mystery *On the Roads of Destiny* (1926) briefly reviews the whole of Lithuanian history, and the tragedy *The Death of Mindaugas*[7] (1930), also speaks of the glorious past but is artistically inferior to his other works. Krėvė based the play *The Son-in-Law* (1939) and the narrative *The Sorcerer* (1939) upon his own experiences in the Lithuanian countryside.

World War II induced changes in Krėvė's life and work. After the Soviet annexation of Lithuania in 1940, he was appointed Minister of Foreign Affairs and assistant to the Prime Minister. He experienced a keen disappointment when, on July 1, 1940, he learned from Molotov in the Kremlin that all of the statements and promises the Soviet Union had made to Lithuania were only a cleverly organized plot. Krėvė's frustration reached its culmination when, on July 14, London radio stations, furnished with information by TASS, the official and only Soviet news agency, broadcast the final results of the staged puppet elections regarding the so-called people's parliaments in the Baltic countries, although the polls were not closed until a day later, that is, July 15. Krėvė abandoned his post and went into hiding. After a few fugitive years in a displaced persons camp in Austria, he joined the faculty of the University of Pennsylvania in 1947. Together with his scholarly work, Vincas Krėvė continued his biblical epic, *The Sons of Heaven and Earth* (Vol. I, 1954; Vol. II, 1963), which is his major work

[6] Skirgaila (c. 1353–1397) was a Lithuanian prince.

[7] Three glorious achievements marked the life of King Mindaugas: under his command the Lithuanian troops defeated the Teutonic knights at Saule in 1236; he expanded his kingdom far to the East, and, finally, Mindaugas deterred the Mongol hordes from moving westward by defeating them at Lyda in 1241. The king and both his sons, Ruklys and Rupeikis, were assassinated in 1263. The date of his birth is unknown.

and which had been in preparation since 1907. The author's death interrupted the projected last volume. The plot revolves around Jesus Christ and the historical persons associated with him.The writer attempted to imitate biblical style, and he succeeded to a great extent. Krēvē's interpretation and dialogue, however, expose mainly his own keen intellect:

> HEROD: I am troubled, Greek. My soul is restless and this is why I have summoned you. You understand much, Greek, more than I, more than anyone else. What you have not gained through reason, you have gained by study.
>
> NICHOLAS: Our great thinker, Socrates, who alone of all men has been called most wise by the eternal gods, has said: —I know only one thing, that I know nothing.
>
> HEROD: Truly words of a wise man. Your wise men are strange, Greek. People say that they know the secrets of heaven and earth, yet they are not proud. They do not boast.
>
> NICHOLAS: Our wise men truly try to understand and to explain the secrets which the gods on Olympus have tried to conceal from the mortal mind, and now many secrets are clear to us, but man's mind is too feeble to know and understand everything.
>
> HEROD: Our wise men do not think this way. They are said to know everything that God knows and still more.
>
> NICHOLAS: I have always believed firmly and constantly that He knows everything and He does not suffer anyone to deny this, my King. And so, I have seen, they always speak of their God by name.
>
> HEROD: They vex me, Greek, and I cannot speak with them. I talk with you and am consoled.
>
> NICHOLAS: I am your physician, my King. I heal not only your flesh, but even your spirit.
>
> (Gerald L. Mayer and Judith Oloskey)

Vincas Krēvē *Works* (1956–1961) comprise six volumes.

In contrast with many other writers and poets, Vincas Mykolaitis-Putinas (1893–1967) was not a struggler but a vacillator both in his political convictions and in his priestly functions. Putinas contributed to every genre of letters. After obtaining his diploma from the theological seminary at Seinai, he did graduate work at a St. Petersburg theological academy. In 1918 he enrolled at the University of Fribourg to study philosophy, literature, and art, earning his Ph.D. for the thesis "L'Esthétique de Vladimir Soloviev" in 1923. He spent a year at the University of Munich attending additional lectures and doing research; then he joined the faculty of the University of Kaunas. From 1940, he taught literature at the University of Vilnius until his retirement in 1954.

While still in the seminary, in 1911, he began to publish his poems under the *nom de plume* of Putinas. His first collection of verses, *The Red Flowers* (1917), was printed in St. Petersburg. In the following volume, *Between Two Dawns* (1927), Vincas Putinas expressed his emotions and his philosophical meditations in a style marked by romanticism and symbolism. This book contains the cycle of six poems "Pessimistic Hymns," written in 1925. The poet compared his life to a poison, from which even the sun and the moon turn away. Some of Putinas' poems are impulsive and contradictory; however, his fluent style and emotional impact make them attractive:

At Midnight

There is but one and only hour—
    The midnight gay,
When to the distant stars above
    You stop and pray.

Forever glowing silent skies
    Such joy impart,
It seems that all the stars descend
    Into your heart.

Entire existence blends 'to one—
    The azure blue,
Which like a calmly rolling sea
    Submerges you.

There is no sky, there is no prayer,
There is no sin;
Whatever word your heart may say—
Heaven will win.

(Nadas Rastenis)

The mediocre mystery *The Vestal Virgin* (1927) and the drama *The Sovereign* (1930) are derived from history. This period of his career is distinct, marked by his inclination toward realism. In 1931, Mykolaitis-Putinas began to write his controversial trilogy, *In the Shadow of Altars* (1933), while on leave in Nice. The novel is autobiographic to some extent, for in the protagonist, Liudas Vasaris, the writer pictured his own concerns. With respect to structure, it is an amalgam of numerous interests and events. The leitmotif conspicuously creates an atmosphere in which Vasaris is unable to remain a true poet and at the same time function as a priest. Putinas tries to shift all the blame on the Church, but unintentionally he shows his hero to be shallow and self-contradictory. The trilogy's blatant charges allured many readers; the ecclesiastical court, however, excommunicated Mykolaitis-Putinas in 1936 because of his flagrant behavior and his obvious affair with a former student, whom he later married.

His novel *The Crisis* (1937) is dedicated to the life of independent Lithuania. This book secured the author a government award in 1939. But when the Red army occupied his country, Putinas, in the volumes *I Greet the Earth* (1950) and *Poetry* (1954), wrote poems favorable to the Soviet regime, employing trite communist slogans. It seems that Putinas regarded this as a false step, for afterward he desisted from the use of propaganda and clichés. In order to avoid dealing with contemporary politics he turned to the past for the subject matter of his next novel, *The Rebels* (1957), which deals with the Lithuanian insurrection of 1863. Mykolaitis-Putinas achieved wide recognition with his literary criticism.

Already during his study of literature in Kaunas, Grènóble, and Paris, Antanas Vaičiulaitis (b. 1906; now in Washington,

D.C.) translated works of Mauriac, Milosz, Unamuno, and Maurois. In 1939, Vaičiulaitis joined the faculty of the University of Lithuania. He compiled textbooks, wrote literary criticism, served as a diplomat, and after World War II, taught as a professor at several American universities. At present he is associated with the Voice of America. Of his numerous books, the more popular are: *Noon at a Country Inn* (1933), short stories derived from lore of the Nemuna River region; *Our Little Sister, Valentina* (1936), a psychological novel portraying the love of two youngsters; *The Path Through a Swamp* (1939), a collection of short stories; *Golden Slipper* (1957), a group of fairy tales, and *Song of Willows* (1966), a series of legends. Vaičiulaitis stresses the psychological element. His characters are very explicit. The story "Noon at a Country Inn" was sparked by Leonardo da Vinci's tale "Monks and a Merchant":

On a warm, sunny day like today and the one we enjoyed yesterday, a man was traveling on foot through the forest. He wore a pair of high, wide boots, velvet trousers, and a jacket of the same material. From time to time he stopped to wipe his face with a red handkerchief.

"Not a soul in sight for miles around!" he sighed dejectedly to himself. "I can already see myself having to fast for a whole year. But wasn't that a dog barking just now?" The traveler quickened his pace and soon arrived at a clearing, where he found a hamlet with an old, tile-roofed inn. The innkeeper, sprawled out in the sun, was lazily stroking his beard, blacker than tar, which flowed down to his waist.

"Please step inside, do!" he said, by way of greeting. "A good table awaits you, and a full jug, too, day or night. And then, it's cooler indoors."

In one corner of the room, which had a low ceiling and smoke-stained walls, lay a tame fox tied to a chain. A middle-aged friar sat beside the table, a book in his hand.

"Ah! A servant of God—this is a pleasure!" said the traveler. "Let me introduce myself. I am Severinas Šendriškis, from the city of Kaunas—though at one time I did reside abroad. I have a house in town, and a daughter. On my wife's side I'm related to His Excellency the Bishop of Žemaičiai—

an image of wisdom, godliness, and every virtue. Whenever
I happen to be in Varniai he graciously offers me his silver
tobacco-box adorned with three rubies. . . . And he pats me
on the shoulder, saying, 'My dear fellow! . . .'"

"Your merits astonish heaven," replied the friar. "In their
light my faults become even more wretched. I'm on a pilgrimage to the Gate of Dawn at Vilnius, to atone for my
sins. . . ."

"Gentlemen," the landlord interrupted them, "and when
will you be wanting to eat?"

"I think we'd rather rest for a bit," said Severinas Šendriškis; and he continued, turning to the friar, "You're on your
way to the Gate of Dawn, did you say? I'm going there myself. Suppose we travel together. . . . What vows are taking
you to Vilnius?"

"It's a selfish vow, my friend. Once I saw a little boy hanging by his shirt from the branch of a tree. The branch was
beginning to break, and the child would certainly have fallen
onto a large heap of stones below. As I hurried to save him, I
made a vow then and there to visit our Lady of the Gate of
Dawn if I could catch him in time. As it turned out, I did
save the rascal from dying; yet I could easily have turned to
the protection of Saint Anthony. As patron of our order, he
was quite available. . . . But I had always longed to make a
pilgrimage to the Gate of Dawn and could never find the
opportunity. It was the very chance I'd hoped for. I explained the whole business to my superior, and he let me go."

"Your motives are as pure as yourself. . . . D'you know?
I made a vow, too. This is how it happened. My daughter
had been taken quite ill—she was even near death. Nothing
seemed to do her the least good, neither doctors nor the finest
medicines we could buy. Then I said to myself: 'I'll walk to
Vilnius to pray to our Lady of the Gate of Dawn if only my
daughter gets well. I'll offer five pure silver candlesticks to
Our Virgin Mother; I'll have masses said in all the churches;
and for a whole half year, at the princely tomb of St. Casimir,
I'll burn a wax taper as thick as the stick I'm carrying.' Almost
at once my daughter began to recover, and now she's even
walking a little, praise God. But where's the landlord now?
You can see from my waistline, I'm no candidate for the
religious life, what? Where are you hiding, landlord?"

"I'm here, gentlemen."

"We're both famished!"

"Well, then, what would you like to eat?"

"What can you offer us?"

"Everything's in the pantry, kind sirs; that is, except for swan's milk."

"Ah, let's see. . . . First bring us two bottles of wine."

"Wine? Hmm. . . . Did you say wine?"

"Yes, wine."

"As old as these log walls are, gentlemen, they've never yet clapped eyes on a bottle of wine."

"Well, do you have mead, then?"

"That I do—all you can drink."

"Would you have a pheasant in your pantry, by any chance?—No? Well, then let's settle for a suckling pig with fruit stuffing.—You don't have that? Very well. It'll have to be plain chicken. Two chickens should do us quite well."

"Dear me, how can I explain?" began the innkeeper. "But only yesterday the hawk carried off my last chicken. And what a plump bird it was!"

"Quite so," remarked Šendriškis drily, pulling in his belt. "Only, that's no comfort to my stomach. But what's that I hear if not a cock crowing?"

"It's a cock of the best breed, gentlemen, such as you never saw in your life," boasted the landlord, tugging at his beard.

"Why didn't you mention it to us before?"

"But sirs, you asked for chicken. How could I guess that you like cockerels?"

"Catch him! He'll do!"

"I'm not sure I can bring myself to part with him. He's been as good as a clock to me for the past ten years."

"I'll give you a whole sovereign for him. I tell you, man, I'm starving, and I won't be able to move from here till I've had a good, substantial meal."

"There's no help for it, then. . . . It's easy for you to say 'sovereign,' but another matter for me to be able to earn it."

Again the cockerel opened his beak and began to crow, either to record the changing weather or to lament his probable doom. His master, clasping his beard with his left hand and holding his right before him, crept stealthily toward the singer, who sat looking at him with mistrust. In reach of the bird, he made a wild clutch at him and fell down flat on the ground. The cockerel flew into the air and, with a shrill cackle, plunged into the kitchen garden. The innkeeper got up, clambered painfully over the fence, and began to dance about amidst the cabbage-heads, entangling himself more and more as he pursued the fowl. At last, safely established on the barn roof, the cockerel flapped his wings about him and scowled fiercely down at the landlord.

"What in heaven's name's the matter with you? Is a devil, or something else, lurking in you? D'you think it's the end of the world if I just want to put you in the oven? Believe me, I've done it many a time to the likes of you, and without half the fuss you're putting up. But no, whatever I do, you won't let me come near you."

"I'll go around to the other side and frighten him from there," suggested Šendriškis from the doorstep.

He picked up a stick, climbed a ladder, and began to wave his "weapon" about in the air. At first the bird couldn't decide what to do; then he beat his wings frantically and flew straight over the innkeeper's head to the ground; next, as fast as his legs could carry him, he scuttered off into the juniper bushes.

"Now we won't even see his tail-feathers," sighed the landlord. "He won't be back till evening, that's sure."

"But what about our meal?"

"Maybe you'd accept some ham, or a piece of wonderfully tasty sausage, seasoned with garlic? Or smoked bacon with black peppers?"

"Man!" cried Severinas. "You don't say a word, and you've got so much of God's bounty here! For heaven's sake, bring it all in, and now."

Bread, meat, bacon, and a comfortable, round jug of mead presently appeared on the table. As Šendriškis zestfully attacked the ham and sausage he did not forget the friar.

"I know that a servant of God must carry nothing on his journey, and that he must eat whatever is offered to him—like a cricket, I might say. Therefore, dear friar, I beg you not to refuse my invitation to this modest fare."

"May Our Dear Lord reward you a hundredfold for your kind heart!" said the friar.

For a time they ate in silence. Then, after Šendriškis had put away some mead and stilled his hunger pangs, he stared at his guest with astonishment.

"But my good man, you're eating meat! That means that you've broken your rule—and that interests me very much. When I was in Kalvarija I made a bet with my friend Fabijonas that some day, sooner or later, I'd find a friar who'd broken his rule. But I didn't expect to win this easily!"

"Please, dear sir, not so fast! You have certainly not won your bet, nor have I broken my rule. Our regulations state quite clearly that we may consume whatever we find along the way—meat, porridge, or plain water."

"Ah, that's a pity! And a disappointment. Now I'm afraid the Dominican will get to heaven the winner. . . . Damn, what a tough sausage this is! You could break your teeth on it, devil take it!"

"Why, you're swearing!" exclaimed the friar, hastily crossing himself.

"But surely, to speak of Satan is to sin—. His name reminds us of hell and its everlasting fire and thus warns us away from the pleasures of sin."

"Please! Sir!—From the ugliness of sin, not pleasures of sin!"

"If you'll allow me—I'm no student of theology, but I do think people wouldn't fling themselves headlong into sin if it were ugly. I ask you, what man ever hopes to marry an ugly woman—and what woman would pursue a repulsive man? Everybody chases after things that are beautiful and pleasant. So surely we must say 'the pleasures of sin.' Otherwise, all sinners would be mere fools!"

"To your remarks about women," began the friar, "I decline to add one word. In my eyes, women are simply snares of the evil spirit, instruments that bring innocent men to their ruin—weather vanes, one might say, on the gables of the churches. . . ."

"I see you've got it in you to preach a fine sermon about women, and it wouldn't surprise me if women, seeing such a black picture of themselves, were to burst into tears. But, let me speak frankly, I wouldn't believe a word you might say."

"Why?"

"Because, as a man of the cloth, you can't possibly know anything about women."

"Ah, but I can always view them from a theoretical standpoint."

"Oh? How could that help anyone? A woman is only interesting as herself. And in the flesh."

The whole time he was talking, Severinas ate on greedily. At last the timid friar could not restrain himself.

"If you're as concerned with your soul as with your body, then heaven's gates have been standing open for you a long time."

"But what in the world is wrong with loving our own body?"

"Everything! The body is the enemy."

"But didn't Our Lord Himself command us: 'Love thy enemy'?"

"Dear sir, you know that the body cannot save you!"

"And why not? Through love of the body, or of the soul, we can be saved."

"O Dear Lord, what heresy!" The friar stood up in his extreme agitation.

"My good friend, in the fullness of time our bodies will rise from the dead and ascend to heaven—if they deserve it. A man who loves his body will never wish to see it perish, but will so act that all he loves may find its way into the Garden of Paradise. . . . But what's that noise? D'you hear it?"

Thunder growled, deep in the woods, and they could see a black storm-cloud gathering in the sky.

As if carved in stone, the trees stood under the heat. The faint chirruping of a bird, and nothing else, could be heard.

Šendriškis stopped eating; the friar had already finished his meal. Then the wind came; it whistled through the gaps in the log walls and flattened the plants beneath the windows. The clouds swelled, heavy and swift, and the trees rustled and moaned. A few drops fell and then ceased. A muffled droning made its way indoors.

The two saw swallows, like black scraps of rags, flying before the wind. Then, all at once, as if someone had ripped the clouds apart, torrents of rain drenched the earth. Thunder followed on the heels of thunder, and lightning continuously slashed the sky. The woods seemed swaddled in muslin, and long fringes of water gurgled down from the ridges of the roof.

Then, as quickly as it had come, the storm blew past.

"Never in my life have I seen such a rain," said the landlord, opening the door.

"Ah!" said Šendriškis, pointing to a tree struck by lightning. "You can even smell the resin!"

The white disk of the sun floated out from the clouds, and the trees, flowers, and bushes stood forth clean and refreshed, as if newly created. The grass, glued before to the ground, righted itself; the puddles glittered; and brooks joyfully ran into the valley.

The air was so cool and refreshing that Severinas decided to have a nap before he set off again on his pilgrimage. When the friar came to waken him, the sun was almost touching the tree-tops of the forest.

"Thanks! I envy you and your journey," said the landlord, as he pocketed the promised sovereign.

The moment the travelers had departed, the cockerel stepped out from the juniper bushes.

"Well, and what do we see here? You've had your feathers washed right and proper, that's for sure," remarked the innkeeper, as he leaned back to await new guests.

Making their way through a fragrant wood of linden-trees, Severinas Šendriškis and the friar came on a swollen brook. After the downpour, its waters had become a river, flowing over the field and bearing torn branches, bushes, and twigs as it plunged on.

"Oh, what a misfortune!" cried Severinas. "I'll never be able to cross this swamp."

"But the water can't be so deep, believe me!" answered the friar. "It'll only come up to your knees."

"You may be right," said Severinas, "but I have a terrible rheumatism in my right leg. How can I cross that stream without getting my feet wet?"

"Don't worry! I'm tremendously strong. In the old days, single-handed, I could easily roll over an ox, I'll carry you across on my shoulders."

Almost at once Šendriškis found himself astride the shoulders of the friar, who walked straight into the water. Then, in the exact center of the stream, the friar halted and spoke anxiously to his friend.

"Tell me, do you have money with you, by any chance?"

"Of course. And I'll give you as much as you want."

"Oh, in that case I am sorry, but I can't carry you farther. My rule strictly forbids me to carry money."

"But my dear friend, I'm the one with the money, not you."

"I know but I'm carrying you and your money, too. Certainly it isn't floating loose in the air. No, there's nothing else to do, you'll just have to come down. If I went on now, I'd be breaking my rule. And what an opportunity that would be for you to win your bet with the Dominican! Please climb off, my friend—maybe God will spare you from rheumatism, this time."

"True, I can't lead you into sin now, can I? Thanks, anyway, for carrying me halfway across the river. Ah, the water's quite warm! Maybe it won't hurt me after all. . . ."

Once on the far bank, Šendriškis waited a while for his leg to begin to ache.

"Hey, there's no pain!" he said cheerfully, after he had stood there for some minutes.

And then the sun began to set in earnest, and the two made their way along the sandy road, till they glimpsed from a hillock the belfries of Vilnius, gleaming far off in the valley. As the evening bells rang forth, both travelers bowed their heads and said the angelus, their eyes resting on the city of their forebears.

(Danguolé Sealey)

After earning his Ph.D. in French from the University of Grènóble, the symbolist Jonas Aistis (b. 1904) moved to the United States, where he is engaged in work at the Library of Congress. Aistis produces intimate lyrical poetry marked with philosophy. His collection *My Sister Struggle* (1951) secured the author a literary award.

Vincas Ramonas (b. 1905; now living in Chicago), started his career with the collection of short stories *Artist Rauba* (1934), then published the novel *Dust in the Red Sunset* (1942) and the three stories in *The Foggy Morning* (1960). His *magnum opus,* however, is the novel *Crosses* (1944), which realistically reveals the conspiracy of the Soviets and the Nazis to destroy Lithuanian independence and their national and moral values:

"Do you know why they deported him to Siberia? Did you hear? What whiskey does! The man had been drinking and began to complain that it was hard to live, that the Bolshevik system was no good. They came in canvas shoes, robbed the leather from all the stores and shipped it to Moscow. No leather, no work for Valiukas, also no bread. And the man blurted out, 'If man is only an animal, then why don't they strip him of his skin too? At least there would be some sort of material for footwear.' So Giruzis informed against him."

Kreivenas hastened away. It was as though he were afraid of being late somewhere.

Grustas shook his finger at him menacingly and went to his own home. Having watered the calves, he left the stable with the pail and was bound for the house. Chancing to glance in the direction of the burial ground, he saw a man there, cutting down the cross. Dropping the pail, he climbed over the fence and ran across the pasture.

"Kreivenas! Man! What are you doing?"

Kreivenas faced about, scowled fiercely and swung the axe harder yet. The cross cracked, leaned farther over and slowly fell to the grass. The crossbeam caught on a linden and, springing off, fell beside the fence.

"What have you done? Was this cross in your way?"

"Yes. It's crowded. So crowded that I'm going to cut down the lindens too. There will be more arable land."

"Do you lack land? Man, man! There will be more than enough, you'll see."

"Why should decayed posts like this be left standing? Finally, is this my land here, or yours? Why do you stick your nose in other people's business?"

"In other people's business! Posts! It may be just a post to you, but people used to gather here, they used to come singing hymns, they used to kneel down and pray. They prayed to God, for everyone, for everyone—for the dead and the living. And for me, and for you."

"For me? I didn't ask them to pray for me and I'm not asking them to."

"You despise the cross. . . . You and others like you. But what kind of cross have you hung on all of us? You, all of you, for whom there is no God. Is it not your children who are slaughtering us now? Here is your own Joseph. . . . Giruzis. He betrays innocent people to the hangmen. He goes to arrest them himself. He arrested Arminas, he arrested Puceta."

"Arminas arrested? Puceta?" Kreivenas drew back.

"He had you denounced too, only Balaika took your part. That's our cross, all these Giruzises. And who is to blame? You and others like you. God knows, maybe we're all to blame. For the sins of all of us. . . . Maybe God will forgive us if we bear this cross patiently. We didn't obey God as we should. And if we did love Him, then we forgot that we must lead our erring sons back to the path of right. We made no effort. We were content with ourselves. But now maybe we'll change for the better. . . ."

"Change for the better. Go on sighing, but there's no reason why I should sigh. Ignorance speaks from your lips. Finally . . . what's the big fuss over? He shouts . . . as though somebody killed a man. . . . Why, tomorrow or the next day, it would've toppled over of its own accord. What's there to shout about? Can't you see that it's all rotten?"

Grustas sighed woefully. That sigh annoyed Kreivenas so much that he jumped forward, tore off the leaden crucifix and held it out to Grustas.

"Take it with you. You can cast yourself a bullet to shoot the devil."

(Milton Stark)

Kreivenas, the hero of *Crosses,* expected social and economic salvation in the Soviet system. This made him a loyal servant of the regime. The moment Kreivenas expresses his disillusion, the communists crucify him.

Jurgis Gliauda (b. 1906; now living in Los Angeles), is familiar to American readers through his novel *House Upon the*

Sand (1951), which discloses the atrocities of the Nazis. His psychological novel *Ora pro nobis* (1952) attempts to elucidate the problem of vengeance. The fictional biography *The Sonata of Icarus* (1961) is dedicated to Mikolajus Konstantinas Čiurlionis (1875–1911), a great Lithuanian composer and painter. Nėlė Mazalaitė (b. 1907; now in Brooklyn, N.Y.) is the Lithuanian Selma Lagerlöf. Her talent lies in her collections of religious and national legends, *The City Which Does Not Exist* (1939), *The King's Fires* (1942), *The Legends of Longing* (1948), and *The Amber Gates* (1952). Mazalaitė has also written the novels *The Moon Called Honey* (1951), *The Path of the Sun* (1954), and *The Harvest Time* (1956). Nature themes, philosophy, and religion pervade five volumes of poetry by A. Tyruolis (Alfonsas Šešplaukis, b. 1909; now in the United States), particularly the collection *Flexuos Years* (1963). Tyruolis obtained his Ph.D. in Innsbruck. Besides his poetry and criticism, he has translated works of Dante, Shakespeare, Goethe, and Rilke.

Henrikas Radauskas (b. 1910; now in Washington, D.C.) cannot be confined within any school or movement, for he is a highly individualistic poet.[8] Radauskas' works form a complex esthetic amalgam of universal values, the genre of which is marked with classical discipline and lucidity. He has published four collections of poetry: *The Fountain* (1935), *Arrow in the Sky* (1950), *The Song of Winter* (1955), and *Lightnings and Winds* (1965). The latter, which tends toward surrealism, is terse and vivid. The poet is employed as a linguistic expert at the Library of Congress.

Many of the best Lithuanian short stories were produced by Stepas Zobarskas (b. 1911; now residing in Woodhaven, N.Y.). He studied languages and literature in Paris, Heidelberg, and New York, was an editor, and has compiled several textbooks. His collections include: *The Good Goblin* (1933), *Behind the Wood* (1936), *The Bird's Fate* (1937), *Strength of a Woman* (1938), *Close to the Earth* (1943), *In the Homeland* (1946),

---

[8] See Rimvydas Silbajoris, "Henrikas Radauskas: Timeless Modernist" in *Books Abroad*, Winter 1969, pp. 50–54.

The Maker of Gods (1961), and *Bobby Wishingmore* (1961).
Zobarskas draws his characters from the common people and
presents them under ordinary circumstances. However, their
calm reason and conscience turn them into extraordinary
heroes. His short story "Monsignor's Footstool" (1944) has been
translated into several languages:

> Carpenter Baltrunas was about sixty, but looked much
> younger. His cheeks glowed with health, his head had
> escaped the fate of many contemporaries and was not bald,
> but handsomely gray. And when, on feast-days and festive
> occasions, he marched, bearing the church banner, round the
> church in the brilliant sunlight, he was conscious that hun-
> dreds of eyes were fixed on him. With a pleasurable feeling
> of excitement in his heart, he knew that there were many
> who envied his good health and especially his skillful hands,
> which were capable of working wonders with wood.
>
> Baltrunas quickly became attached to each priest who
> came tò the parish, but to none so strongly as to Monsignor
> Labutis. For Monsignor Labutis was a priest with a golden
> heart, pure as spring water and merciful as the Good Samari-
> tan. His hair was even grayer than the carpenter's, and when
> he crossed the church-yard, holding his hat in his hand, his
> head gleamed from afar, like a white clover blossom. The
> very earth seemed to light up with his presence and his kind
> smile. He had only one shortcoming, that is, if a Monsignor
> can be said to have any human failings at all: he was very
> diminutive in stature.
>
> The carpenter would not soon forget the first mass Mon-
> signor Labutis said upon his arrival in the parish. He had to
> open the door of the Tabernacle to take down the Mon-
> strance, and he could not reach it. He stood on tiptoe, and
> stretched himself to the full extent of his stature, and even
> his neck and ears grew red as fire, but he was still unable to
> touch the Monstrance. On that very day the sacristan was ill,
> and Baltrunas had volunteered to replace him. Not knowing
> how best to help the priest, the carpenter crossed himself,
> seized the first piece of board that came into his hands, and
> ran up to the altar. He shoved it under the Monsignor's feet,

and since it was too thin, supported it from beneath with his clenched hands. Monsignor balanced upon it and, without the slightest difficulty, grasped the Monstrance. On that day the carpenter vowed to present the church with such a footstool as the Archbishop himself did not have in his resplendent cathedral.

The carpenter set to work the very next week. He found in his attic a piece of oak, which was very well adapted for his purpose, and began to fashion a footstool for Monsignor. He adorned it with carvings representing scenes from the Holy Scriptures. On one side, he carved the heads of the lion and the lamb, to depict the might and the love of the Holy Faith; on the other side, he made a large chalice in a halo of rays, and farther on a number of flowers in full bloom and creepers, and the sacrifice of Isaac, or rather the sacrificial altar, from which thick clouds of smoke were rising. The execution was admirable, for carpenter Baltrunas had spared no pains and had applied all his skill.

It is hardly necessary to say that Monsignor was highly pleased and, in the presence of the church council, gave free vent to his admiration.

"It's a true work of art," declared the priest. "Really, I am almost afraid to step onto such a masterpiece."

"You embarrass me, Monsignor! It is a mere nothing," protested the carpenter humbly.

But when Monsignor shook his hand, the carpenter almost burst into tears, so deeply was he moved. He returned to his house late, for on that day he dined at the Rectory. The sky was full of stars. Giddy with his success, Baltrunas trod on air. "Every time," he reflected, "that Monsignor stepped on the footstool to reach the Monstrance, he would be reminded of me, poor miserable sinner. And if I should happen to die first, no one would pray for me so much as he, God's aged minister, and his prayers would mount directly to the Lord's throne on high."

But quite suddenly the Bishop transferred Monsignor Labutis to another parish. There, it was said, life would be much easier and more agreeable for the aged priest; the church there was a true work of art, the parish much richer;

besides, there Monsignor would have the aid of two younger priests, and he would not have to wear himself out with confessions and sermons, as he would have to preach only on the more solemn church festivals.

The carpenter wondered whether he should offer Monsignor his newly-carved footstool as a going-away gift. But then, he thought, the altar in that church might be lower, or there might be a permanent step attached to it, covered with a rich cloth; besides, Baltrunas himself had entered his gift in the parish inventory, and it was hardly possible to delete the entry now. So, Monsignor departed without the carpenter's gift, albeit deeply lamented and given a send-off through the green ceremonial arch erected for the occasion.

Monsignor's successor was a somewhat younger priest, almost as old as the carpenter and as small as Monsignor Labutis. No smile lit up his face. The wizened, irascible, grim minister of God aroused, from the very first day, not a little fear in the church servants and the rectory maids. His eyes, the sharp glint of which was further intensified by the silver eyeglasses he wore, seemed to penetrate everywhere, trusting no one and taking everyone to task. The carpenter himself, who was no coward, did not feel very comfortable when the new priest fastened his piercing eyes on him and commanded him to bring the cash-book in which was entered the money collected during mass. This money was in the special care of the carpenter. Summoning several more parishioners, he most scrupulously counted it and deposited it, every penny of it, in the parish cashbox. The Monsignor had always trusted him blindly and had never taken the trouble to verify whether the money had been correctly counted and entered in the cash-box. Baltrunas took umbrage at such marked distrust, but he was unwilling to start a quarrel with the newcomer. He felt uneasy, as he looked at the tightly compressed lips and protruding chin, and when the priest directed his glance at him, Baltrunas grew hot all over, as if he had committed some fault, and would have willingly sunk through the ground, if only he had not had to face the priest. But the carpenter soon recovered his spirits.

"Just wait," he thought, "when you discover who I am,

you won't be so grim," and raising his footstool, Baltrunas said:

"This is my handwork."

"Is that so?" replied the priest, hardly casting a glance at his masterpiece. "So, you're a handicraftsman, as well?"

"A very poor one, Father, but still I can make anything I set my mind to, for myself and for others, in my moments of leisure."

"Very good."

The priest's voice was devoid of interest, rough, and did not show the least surprise or admiration. Though the carpenter still held in his hands the fondest child of his fancy, the priest paid no more attention. He went down on his knees, prayed for a short while, and then set about his preparations for mass.

If someone had driven a knife deep into his back, carpenter Baltrunas would not have felt such excruciating pain. At that moment, his heart contracted, and he felt that he could never love that priest. He began to appear in the sacristy more and more rarely, and he called at the Rectory only when the rector was absent. Shortly before Christmas, when the priest began his annual visitation of his parishioners, Baltrunas failed to give a dinner in his honor, as was his custom in other years. He merely gave the rector, the organist, the sacristan, and the others a bushel of corn each, wishing to emphasize in this way that he had no intention of making any distinction between this priest and the generality of mankind. The carpenter rejoiced at the thought that this action of his would irritate the priest, but the latter was perfectly unmoved. He looked through his glasses as calmly and as grimly as if he had been bountifully gifted. He expressed his thanks politely, blessed the home and departed to visit his other parishioners.

"What a queer old man!" muttered Baltrunas under his breath, looking at the fresh sledge-tracks. For a short space of time the sledge-bells could be still heard, but soon silence returned again. The snow-covered trees stood calmly, and from time to time a cloud of light snow-flakes descended from their branches.

Suddenly it appeared to Baltrunas that if the rector had
been more friendly, he could have asked him whether the
carpenter's granaries had been so soon emptied, and whether
that was the reason why his gift had been so small. Baltrunas'
heart would then have been gladdened and he would have
doubled or trebled his bounty. But no, the rector had not
even deigned to notice it, as he had not deigned to examine his
footstool, although every time he said mass, he mounted it.

"So you hate me, you old codger. Just you wait! I'll get
even with you, then we'll see who'll come out on top, you or
I," the carpenter said to himself.

From that day on the carpenter became obsessed by the
thought of how he could best revenge himself on the rector.
You could not give him a beating, that was obvious, for no
matter how much you disliked him, he was still a priest, and
an old priest at that. You could not spit in his face, either.
And Baltrunas ruminated day and night, in impotent rage,
until he was struck by a sudden idea—an idea of such brilliance that he hugged himself with joy.

It was the eve of the feast of St. John. The carpenter
entered the church, and seizing the moment when all the
altars were decorated and when the young girls engaged in
the arrangement of the flowers and the garlands had left, he
stole into the sacristy. Having assured himself that no one
saw him, Baltrunas sought out his footstool, and looked long
and lovingly at the sacrificial altar and at the flowers which
could have been improved upon, but then there was no sense
in trying to refurbish an old thing like that. The bricks of the
sacrificial altar and the wreathing smoke had been defaced
in places, but on the whole, the footstool was still very lovely.
And that such a masterpiece be trod by such a rector!

"No matter, I made it, and I can destroy it," thought the
carpenter as he tried to wrench a foot off.

It was no easy task. The oak leg held firm, and Baltrunas
felt such pain in his heart, as if he were rending, limb by
limb, a living lamb, and not a mere thing of wood. Still, his
resentment prevailed over his better feelings, and the carpenter wrenched off all the four feet, one after another. To pre-
vent the church servants from noticing the damage, he lightly
tacked them in place, so that the footstool would have col-

lapsed under even the weight of a little child. After that he replaced it and went down on his knees, as guiltlessly as could be, before the altar.

Not a word of his design did the carpenter say to his wife or his children at home. It would be a fine sight, he thought, when his grim reverence mounted the footstool and it flattened out under him. Naturally, the priest would come to no harm, but his very eyeglasses would rise in rage. Then he could stretch his hands, standing on tiptoe, and try to reach the Monstrance! The disgrace would be less on an ordinary Sunday, but the next day was a festival day! Many neighboring priests would be present, and big crowds of people from the surrounding parishes would be there.

The carpenter slapped his thighs and set about his preparations for going to church. The bells rang out. Dressed in his Sunday best, Baltrunas hastened to take up his regular place near the high altar. His wife and his children were at their prayers on the side reserved for women.

Followed by four altar-boys, the priest emerged from the sacristy and the organ pealed out loudly under the lofty vault. The carpenter bowed his head and raised it only when the church choir was singing the words of the hymn, "Bend ye your knees." Suddenly his eyes rested on the head of the celebrating priest, which was as white as a clover blossom, and a hot wave of agony swept over him. Merciful God! The priest at the altar was not the rector, but a visitor, none other than Monsignor Labutis!

Only then did Baltrunas feel all the enormity of his prank suggested by the very Father of Evil himself. On his knees, beside the large painting of the Holy Virgin holding her heavenly child on her lap, with gray clouds rolling under her feet and golden stars glistening above her head, the carpenter could hardly breathe. The good Prelate had aged even more. His voice quavered, and when he bowed to kiss the altar, the Holy Ghost itself seemed to bow in the likeness of a silver dove. And when this gentle old man mounted the footstool and lost his foothold, who could say whether he would not tumble down and break his leg? And perhaps he would have the Holy Host in his hands and in falling would drop it? And suppose they discovered that he, Baltrunas, was responsible?

Well, even if they did not, could one hide one's evil deeds from the allseeing eye of God, Who, quite likely, would whisper to His beloved Monsignor in his sleep that he, Baltrunas, who bore the banner in the church processions, who had been so implicitly trusted by the priest, had played that mean trick?

The mass continued. Monsignor Labutis faced the congregation to intone "Dominus vobiscum," and to Baltrunas his eyes seemed to say, "A very good morning to you." The faithful, with such a visitor in their midst, prayed with joyful fervor. The choir sang more vigorously than it had done for a long time. The organist, with coat-tails, thumped with his hands and pumped with his feet, conducting the choir with his head. The bright sunlight poured through the stained-glass windows, and rainbows arched over star-spangled altar tops. "Et cum spiritu tuo," rolled from the lowly earth to the firmament in a mighty surge.

"Good Heavens, what have I done, what have I done!" whispered the carpenter, bathed in perspiration; and he glanced at the church clock, the hands of which moved forward inexorably.

His temples throbbed.

The carpenter watched every gesture of the priest narrowly, harkened to every sound the rustling pages of the missal made, and he felt his blood chilling in his veins from sheer terror. Now! Now!

One of the altar-boys bent down on one knee, proceeded to the sacristy, re-emerged carrying the footstool, and stood by the altar waiting for Monsignor's nod. At that moment, in which the priest turned his glance upon the dutiful altar boy, the carpenter sprang to his feet, and elbowing those in his way aside, dashed up to the altar and wrested the footstool from the altar boy's hands.

All the congregation looked up in amazement. The altar-boy drew aside in fear, thinking that the carpenter had taken leave of his senses. Even Monsignor Labutis lifted his eyes in mild surprise, but on recognizing the well-known features of the handicraftsman, smiled benevolently, glanced down, and mounted upon the footstool, which the carpenter held firmly with his hands.

When mass was over, carpenter Baltrunas decided to go to the sacristy and to make a clean breast of it. The unexpected turn of events had shaken him to the core. He began to think that God himself had preserved him from committing a crime, by inspiring Monsignor to celebrate high mass. Timidly, like a child making its first tottering steps, the carpenter entered the sacristy; his face turned scarlet as he saw the footstool with the broken legs next to the cabinet where the amices were kept. Both priests had already said their prayers, and when they noticed the carpenter, the rector rose, and walking up to him, extended his hand.

"Thank you very much, Baltrunas, for saving my confrater from a serious mishap. The poor old man would have had a bad tumble but for you."

Uttering those words, he shook hands with Baltrunas and adjusted his eyeglasses, through which his small, active, penetrating eyes gleamed brightly.

"He has saved me a second time," responded Monsignor with a laugh.

"Yes, it was my fault," whispered Baltrunas, restraining his tears with difficulty. "At times the devil takes a man's mind away."

"No fault of yours," said the rector comfortingly. "It was made such a long time ago."

"But what a beautiful piece of work!" added Monsignor.

"Yes, my parish can boast of true artists."

"No, no, I am no artist," answered the carpenter modestly, though in his heart of hearts he felt great joy, and decided to waive further explanations. Both priests suddenly appeared to him so kind, so dear, so worthy of love and veneration that he kissed, in turn, both their hands and said in a voice ringing with determination:

"Tomorrow I will set to work and I will make a new footstool. . . ."

He wanted to say that he would make a footstool such as he had made for no one up to then, but having recollected that such a remark might offend Monsignor, he added:

". . . a footstool that will never break."

(Viktoras Kamantauskas)

In the field of juvenile literature the name of Vytas Tamu-laitis (b. 1913, now living in Canada) is well known. He began his literary career as a student and has written six volumes: *The Rabbit's Memoirs* (1935), *The Spring Is Coming* (1937), *Vytukas' Journal* (1937), *A Night on the Nemunas River* (1938), *The Return* (1948), and *Voyages of the Musician Cricket* (1960).

Eduardas Mieželaitis (b. 1919) started his legal studies in 1939, but they were interrupted during the Soviet invasion when he plunged into politics. Now he is a deputy to the Supreme Soviet of the USSR and the chairman of the Writers Union of occupied Lithuania. In the volumes of poems *Lyrics* (1943) and *The Wind from the Native Land* (1946), Mieže-laitis absorbed national traditions, described the landscape, and paid tribute to the regime he supports. According to Afanasi Salynsky, Mieželaitis' poetry "provides us with the image of a man whose thoughts and sentiments cannot but thrill us. . . . He is a communist in his daring ideas, his open-heartedness, his love for the people around him and his hatred of their enemies."[9]

Meanwhile, Mieželaitis traveled throughout Europe and the United States, where he met Robert Frost, Arthur Miller, and Allen Ginsberg. In keeping with socialist realism, Mieželaitis wrote the political epic *The Poem of Brotherhood* (1954), in which collective farmers of three "brotherly" republics con-struct a mutual power station. His book of verse *Man* (1961) purports to represent the inflexibility of a Soviet citizen and the optimistic philosophy of socialism:

> Here I stand on the globe of our planet,
> Firmly holding the orb of the sun.
> So between these two spheres I'm standing,
> Joining the earth and sun.
> Mental strata, the brain's treasures,
> As profound as our planet's deposits.
> From them, as if it were coal I were mining,

[9] Afanasi Salynsky, "Man's Vocation," *Soviet Literature* VI (1962), 151.

As if ore from my mind I were smelting,
I produce mighty seagoing vessels,
And I bind the land with my railways,
As extensions of birds I make aircraft
And develop from lightning my rockets.
From the depths of my head they issued,
From that spheroid shaped like the earth.
Yet my head's a solar spheroid
With felicity luminescent,
Bringing life to this earth, our planet,
So that everywhere mankind can live.

What's the world without me?
With no life,
Slightly deformed and wrinkled, that sphere
Wandered aimless throughout the vast Cosmos
And it saw in the moon its reflection,
Oh, so dead,
And hideous, too!

Then the earth in its anguish made me.
In a moment of sadness the earth
Made my head in the form of a sphere,
So it's shaped like the sun and our planet.
Tho' the scale of it's small, yet it proved
To be greater by far than our earth.
In submission the world took from me
All the beauty I had to give.
First I was conceived by the earth,
I then moulded all the earth anew,
Made our world more magnificent still,
Of a beauty never surpassed.

Here I stand on the globe of our planet,
Firmly holding the orb of the sun,
Cosmic bridge from the sun to our planet.
And through me
Sun to earth comes descending,
While the earth to the sun reaches upwards.

And round me both these spheres rotate.
Bright that merry-go-round is whirling.

All achievements of art, all workmanship,
Are brought forth by these hands of mine—
And the cities all turn round me, too,
And the houses I've built,
All those asphalted squares,
All those bridges crowded with people and cars,
Those great liners, those aircraft, all move around me,
All the tractors and lathes move around me
And round me all the rockets in orbit move. . . .

So I stand—
Majestic, wise and steadfast,
Broad of shoulder and potent.
The bright sun I've encompassed, so great is my stature.
I project on our planet
The smiles of sunlight
Both eastwards and westwards,
To north and to south.
So I stand—
For I am Man,
A Communist.

(Tom Botting)

In 1962, Mieželaitis was awarded the Lenin Prize for the book. His sketches and reminiscences make up *The Lyrical Studies* (1964) and *The Bread and the Word* (1965).

An outstanding example of the striving immigrant writer is Algirdas Landsbergis (b. 1924; now in Richmond Hill, N.Y.). He was a dishwasher, gasoline station attendant, ditch digger, and lathe operator, until he completed his graduate studies in comparative literature at Columbia University and joined the faculty of Fairleigh Dickinson University. He gained popularity with his first novel, *The Journey* (1955), a thorough psychological analysis of an immigrant. In the three-act play *Wind in the Willows* (1956), he recaptures Lithuania's glorious past in the sixteenth century. The drama *Five Posts in a Market Place* (1956) portrays a tragic conflict between Lithuanian patriots and the Soviet occupants. The same motif dominates the volume of stories *The Long Night* (1956). In 1964, Landsbergis wrote the allegorical play *The Beard* and two years later the play *Farewell, My King* (1966). The plays of Algirdas Landsbergis have been performed on minority stages from coast to coast. His works contain profound, at times complex, philosophy and sharply contrasted situations; they frequently employ caustic comparisons, irony, and paradox. Landsbergis' comedy *The School for Love* (1965), which is illustrated by an excerpt below, focuses on Lithuanian refugees who try to discover the true America in New York, and then exhibit a Quixotic fanaticism in their desire to change it by teaching love, obedience, and good etiquette:

> *Oken is seen sitting by the mannequin, looking back-stage; Adenoid awakes from her faint on the four-poster and begins taking off her wig; Libidstone sits inside the tub, meditating.*

ANGEL: End of another day shift. Fake moonlight is about to rise over artificial lakes. Soon canned violins will sprinkle candied notes, trained cows will moo in unison, tinsel stars will blink, and three thousand couples will be taught how to hold hands—for the last time!

> *During his talk he checks and camouflages his fellow conspirators, unseen by them. He throws a drape over the mannequin to hide Oken; he piles up pillows on the four-poster to conceal Adenoid; he pulls the shower-curtain around Libidstone.*

ANGEL (*to audience*): Listen! This morning I passed a small green house with dark green shutters. A house like that —that's all I wanted; a little house and peace. Didn't you all?—You chuckle at me—a little man who collects pieces of paper. I say—watch out for little men who discover what hells they have been carrying within. You may return my stamps now, hand me my little house on a platter—it is too late. Even revenge, simple, sweet revenge is not enough anymore. In these spaces of America, how my hell, how my ambition has stretched far and wide. Now the prize is everything. This roof will open soon, the walls will crumble, the collapsing dome will bury the whale. And then I'll be on top. I'll turn this Babylonian tower into another school—for thrift, sobriety and strictest decency! And then, on top, perhaps you'll find me strong . . . and handsome. There will be no more chuckling!

> *One more look and the Angel goes out. An instant of complete silence, which is punctured by a yawn from Oken's hiding place. His stretching arm becomes visible, then his face. Having established that the coast is clear, he opens his cake box, slices a piece with a pocket knife, and begins to munch on it. Attracted by the rustling, Adenoid sticks out her inquisitive nose. Seeing the cake, she licks her lips, lifts her eyes and swallows deeply. She gives a conspiratorial cough and, remembering her lesson, covers her face up to her eyes. Oken jumps back behind his drape and then peeks out.*

OKEN *(whispers)*: What peepers! Wait a minute—I've seen them somewhere!

> *They both drop curtains from their faces.*

OKEN-ADENOID *(simultaneously)*: It's you!—What are you doing here:

> *Pause.*

OKEN *(bows in mock-ceremony)*: Will you honor me by visiting my parlor?

ADENOID *(having already taken a couple of steps toward Oken)*: Shall I?

OKEN: Feel at home. Late homework?

ADENOID: Not allowed to tell.

OKEN: Same here.

ADENOID: Any idea who gives instructions?

OKEN: Not the faintest!

ADENOID *(removing a long blond wig-hair from her shoulder)*: All I can say is, he has some weird ideas on fashion.

OKEN: He didn't say we shouldn't have some fun while we wait.

ADENOID *(suspiciously)*: How do you mean that?

OKEN: Join the picnic, have some cake.

ADENOID: Oh, cake . . . sorry.

OKEN: It's good—nine-layer.

ADENOID *(assuming the position for a* Vogue *front cover):* I'm a model. *(More militantly.)* That's why I'm here!

The light switches to Libidstone's section.

LIBIDSTONE: Why *am* I here? Conspiracy? That's only the uppermost layer. How many layers beneath? These strange noises, subliminal rumblings—will they tell me? Darkness is closer to the center of things—I'm in darkness—hence, I'm closer to the center of things. Is liberation in burial? A dazzling thought!

The light switches to the middle section. Diana walks in, bare-footed, weary and dazed. She is still in her "picture" costume and is carrying her 1919 shoes in her hand. She sits down on the four-poster and fingers a tress of her hair with skeptical fingers. Steps are heard. Oken motions to Adenoid and they both quickly hide under the drape by the mannequin. Libidstone draws the shower curtain around himself. Gabriel enters stage-left, a flashlight in his hand. The flashlight catches Diana's foot.

GABRIEL: Sorry, Miss. . . . *(As his flashlight wanders over Diana, with a voice full of disbelief.)* . . . This section is closed for the night. *Who* are you?

DIANA *(realizing that Gabriel does not recognize her, because of the darkness and her disguise—nonchalantly):* And who are you?

GABRIEL: I work here . . . wait—*you're* supposed to answer *my* question.

His last sentence does not carry much authority. He studies her silhouette intently.

DIANA *(gets up):* Well, since you're closing up, I'd better be going. I wouldn't like to get a nice guy like you into trouble.

GABRIEL *(taking a long look at her):* No trouble. Could you stay a moment longer?

DIANA: Why?

GABRIEL: You remind me of someone. A photograph of a young woman dressed just like you in my godmother's album. A funny thing to remember, isn't it, when I remember so little from home?

DIANA: Do I look that old?

GABRIEL: No! Young and beautiful—that's how she looked. But you're right, by now she would be at least a hundred years old. Say, you're not some ball of mist; I mean, a spook; my boss has a spray against them.

DIANA *(beginning to enjoy the mix-up):* Thanks for the warning. I may be your fairy godmother. If you look behind the four-poster you'll find an album with one photograph missing—I've stepped out from it.

GABRIEL *(automatically makes a step toward the place she indicated, stops, wheels around, smiles):* You almost fooled me!

Diana begins to laugh and he joins her.
(More seriously.) Your voice—I can swear I've heard it somewhere. Tell me about yourself.

Light switches to Oken and Adenoid.

OKEN: Tell me everything: your measurements; your bowling score, your social security number. Your measurements. . . .

ADENOID: Ah, it was a lovely, lovely world I used to live in. A very gala world, a real Mecca for a young woman. It smelled nice, too. I lived luxuriously in my self-fitting bra. My filmy chiffons were pure flattery. And I was so smart to look my prettiest in fluid-line silk—blue mist, peach prelude, pool aqua, crystal pink. Nine out of ten top designers said I looked divine in my caftan coats. Yes, mine was the shape of three years ago, of two years ago, of one year ago. . . . But *not* of this year!

OKEN: That's a dirty shame! Why not?

ADENOID: Someone has torn off my caftan coat, pulled off my sheath skirt, wrenched off my stiffened flirtatious petticoat, and exposed my tiny natural waist to the cold world. *(Militantly).* That's why I'm here!

OKEN: The man who did it should be shot. But I sort of envy him. . . .

ADENOID *(with some indignation):* Mr. Oken, do you want me to leave?!

Light switches to Libidstone.

LIBIDSTONE: To leave this darkness will be like being born again. Oh, the pressure of the fat man's hand—power and confidence—like mother and father sublimated into a single palm. This dark, dark womb around me! Listen, bookworms, wherever you are—one dark womb is worth more than forty thousand books!

Light switches to Diana and Gabriel.

DIANA: One fairy godmother knows more than all the books in the world. And they were made to be confided in.

GABRIEL: I will confide in you because you remind me of her.

DIANA: Of whom?

GABRIEL: The girl I love.

DIANA: Who is she?

GABRIEL: She works here. Diana's her name.

DIANA *(her voice loses its bantering tone):* How do you know you—love her?

GABRIEL: That's *all* I know. War scorched the milk off my lips. War's rush, mud, smoke was unreal; but the short stops, warm touches, fast lips—these were, these are, the only real things I've ever known. What else *is* there?

DIANA: Is this now—another short stopover?

GABRIEL: No, no—this is quite different! Like a fresh wound. *(Searches for words.)* Did you ever see how a tree is grafted?

DIANA: Yes, in Pennsylvania.

GABRIEL: Back home, in East Europe, I was like a very young, ungrafted tree. Some girls had leaned against me and had left a hint of their perfume, a touch of their fingers. But ever since I've seen Diana, I'm like a tree that has been grafted.

DIANA: I understand you. . . .

GABRIEL: Will she? She never seemed to listen.

DIANA: She may have been too busy watching for a luxury liner.

GABRIEL: But the School has no windows to the harbor.

DIANA: This fairy tale may explain it to you. Once upon a time, back in Pennsylvania, a little girl saw a postcard of a luxury liner—a gold-trimmed cloud of a ship. A former neighbor, who had struck it rich, mailed it to her family to make them envious. The little girl couldn't pull her eyes away from the ship. Her father pressed the postcard with his miner's fingers, and his thumb-print remained on the white hull, indelible. It was then that the little girl vowed to herself she'd leave the mining town and get on that ship. And she's been carrying the postcard with her ever since.

GABRIEL: And then?

DIANA: The ship sank, like soggy gingerbread. She took out her postcard.

Diana takes out a postcard from her 1919-dress pocket. She tore off the luxury liner.

She tears off most of the postcard, leaving only a small piece of it.

And she will keep the only real part of it—an old miner's fingerprint.

GABRIEL: It's a beautiful fairy tale. But what should *I* do?
Diana takes a long look at him, glances away from him, returns her eyes to him.

DIANA: *(her voice caresses now):* Tell her.

GABRIEL: When?

DIANA: Right now.
She slowly takes off the wig. Astonished recognition in Gabriel's eyes. Light switches to Oken and Adenoid.

ADENOID *(with affection):* Tell me, pretty please.

OKEN: You can't be interested in Atlantic City conventions—you who had your pool aquas and pink crystals.

ADENOID: But I just *love* to hear you talk about it. The smoke-filled rooms, the men sweating in corridors, the convention nights. How exotic, exciting! Especially the sweat!

OKEN: What's so big about sweat?

ADENOID: I never had any, like I never had cake. I lived inside a deodorant tube! And you, you've led such an exciting life. Sweat!

OKEN: Your interest thrills me—imagine, it makes even perspiration inspiring. Will you believe me that I aimed much higher; that I didn't aim to stop in a union lawyer's shoes?

ADENOID: I'm sure you did. Through cigarette smoke, through sweat, you reached higher.

OKEN: I used to get cakes on special occasions, with little figurines on top—a wedding that was called off, you know—and I always dreamt of getting one with a State Governor or a Senator on top—Big politics, that's where my secret heart is.

ADENOID: You should make good at it.

OKEN: Funny, coming from you, it doesn't sound so impossible. I haven't felt that confident since I was a law student. I was reaching for a Napoleon—you might say—and somehow I ended up with a doughnut. I woke up to see that I was sitting in somebody's palm and *that* somebody—in somebody else's, and so on.

He takes her hand and puts his fist on it.

There's only one way: you must be right next to the top guy. Like here. Whoever is next to the big guy here, has a whale of a luck.

As he gazes into the distance, she puts her hand on his fist in her palm. He suddenly becomes aware of her motion and clasps his other hand over hers. The light switches to Libidstone.

LIBIDSTONE: A whale! Could I be sitting in the entrails of a whale? To stay within the whale and to submit—is that the answer? Darkness and peace. No more need to strive, to search, to wade through footnotes—only to be, to be in the warm inside.

Yawns.

An unknown feeling floods my heart—gratitude. To that big, fat man.

Yawns.

To raise my hand against him now?

Yawns very deeply.

No . . . inside the whale . . . very grateful. . . .

Light to Diana and Gabriel. They hold hands.

DIANA: Where are you taking me now?

GABRIEL: To a birch grove in my childhood. Step softly—some angels are dozing against the trees. In the sun-drenched distance, my father is mowing the hay—he's very young.

DIANA: How do I look?

GABRIEL: Pigtails, upturned nose, a smudge on your cheek.

Diana raises her hand to strike him in mock indigna-

tion. He catches her hand in the air. She fits her palm against his.

DIANA: Next to your childhood I'll place mine. A cluster of linden-trees in Pennsylvania.

GABRIEL: Your age?

DIANA: Early spring.

GABRIEL: The season?

DIANA: Fall.

GABRIEL: Let me watch you grow up.

DIANA: It's seven falls later. I've kicked through high school as a drum majorette, May Queen, member of honor societies. The baton and the crown decide my future. For me—it will be acting fame; for father and mother—a husband with five bathrooms and gilded faucets. The soot of the mines keeps haunting them. I go to New York, immense New York. For three years I storm the theaters, and get tired. And now I'm here.

GABRIEL: Do you love me?

She puts her head on his shoulder.

DIANA: My head has found its place. That is the greatest miracle.

The roof opens slowly. Pale moonlight colors the conspirators.

GABRIEL: A miracle!

DIANA: But it's not supposed to open now—they use the artificial sky for the night shift.

GABRIEL: Whatever it is, it's right on time.

He takes her ring finger.

From this moonlight I'll make you a ring. . . .

Light to Oken and Adenoid.

ADENOID: *(notices in the new moonlight the glitter of the ring on Oken's finger):* A ring!

OKEN *(unsuccessfully trying to hide his ring):* Damn moonlight. . . .

ADENOID *(shocked):* You're married!

OKEN: I guess a guy can't kick the truth around too long.

ADENOID: You lied!

OKEN: No! Every word came straight from the middle of my heart. My wife, she never gave a hoot about my work, my

ambitions, as you do. She's a Sing-Sing and Siberia rolled
into one, with a bit of Jersey City thrown in.

ADENOID: How horrible!

OKEN: I had even forgotten to try to get out. But here,
I've got a new feeling, a feeling that everything is possible.

ADENOID: You, too? Oh, Joseph!

OKEN: You called me Joseph!

ADENOID: Yes—Joseph, Joseph, Joseph!

A waltz of sweet violins floats in.

OKEN: I've been liberated! Like I had gone to the head of
the Statue of Liberty and, suddenly, the whole world is at my
feet, laughing!

ADENOID: I'll share your liberty.

*She rips the cake box open, grabs a piece of cake and
starts gobbling it up.*

OKEN: I've seen oodles of mouths covered with cake
crumbs, but none can beat yours.

ADENOID: Oh, Joseph.

Takes another slice.

Love is—sweet.

OKEN: School for Love, I've an announcement to make. I
thank you for bringing this woman into my life! To be fair
and square—I thank you, big, fat man in charge. Without
you—no school! without school—Siberia.

*Suddenly, the sweet violin waltz veers into a blaring
Sousa march.*

OKEN and ADENOID: The signal!

They look at each other and both shake their heads.

OKEN: I'm with you! We won't kick someone who
brought us together.

*First faint rumblings and crashes in the distance.
Adenoid and Oken hide under the drape. More rumblings and crashes punctuated by the Angel's hysteri-
cal laughter. Light on Diana and Gabriel, holding
hands.*

DIANA: That noise! What can it be?

GABRIEL: Some new sound effect.

DIANA: They've never used it before.

GABRIEL: All things are new—because we're in love.
Lights dim. Noises multiply, become louder. Light on Angel in the background, standing on the steps.
ANGEL *(softly):* Friends.
Getting no response, louder.
Allies!
Losing patience.
It's on! Out, out, to work!
Hearing no answer, Angel dashes down, stage-left. He tears off the drape from the mannequin: Oken and Adenoid are kissing each other, oblivious of him or anything else. Angel clutches his head with his hands in despair and runs forward. He collides with the four-poster and notices Gabriel and Diana in an embrace. Angel raises his arms in rising despair and dashes to the next section. He tears open the closed shower curtain—Libidstone is sound asleep. Angel emits a yell of accumulated rage and turns on the water.
LIBIDSTONE *(jumps out blinded, half-awake):* Water! The whale has swallowed water!
Angel stares at him in surprise.
ANGEL: He's nuts—they've all gone nuts! But even if the whole world goes crazy—I'll do it alone!
Angel dashes out stage-right. Then pandemonium erupts. Several musical scores blare out, trying to drown each other. Petals of flowers flutter down gently, interrupted by bursts of confetti. A violinist descends from the ceiling, serious and engrossed in his music. Doves glide by; cows moo and rumble across the stage; shadows of love students flit by in panic; bicycles-built-for-two collide and fall apart; little cupids ascend and descend, together with signs proclaiming the slogans of the School for Love.
LIBIDSTONE *(dripping wet, runs to the front of the stage and falls on his knees):* Praised be the whale!

curtain

A fresh and original talent is discernible in the prose of Vytaute Žilinskaitē (b. 1930; resides in Vilnius). She graduated in journalism from the University of Vilnius in 1955, then for eleven years worked as an editor of the periodical *Youth Columns*. Simultaneously, she produced the volume of poetry *Don't Stop, My Moment* (1961) and humorous stories in the book *Not at the First Look* (1962). The narrative *My Hatred Is Stronger* (1964) concerns the Nazi invasion of Lithuania. *I Also Have Tended Goats* (1965), has a well-devised plot, skillfully treated with wit. Only in 1966 did Žilinskaitė give up journalism and devote herself to literature professionally. Her collections *The Angel Above a City* (1967) and *Love for the Society* (1968) contain humor, satire, and parody, but the story *The Strength of Liars* (1968) deals with a juvenile fantasy. Vytaute Žilinskaitė realizes that this genre isn't characteristic of a woman; however, she is extremely proficient and critics call her work intellectual. The equanimity of English satire fascinates the writer, for she cannot deride without becoming involved.

In the story "Merry-go-round" her irony focuses upon typical, organized contests among individual workers, teams, and specially formed shock brigades, who carry out all assignments prescribed by the Soviet government at the greatest possible speed. The story shows, with delightful humor, that what might theoretically be recorded as a dazzling accomplishment becomes, in the practical order, a singular absurdity.

Merry-go-round

The operator was bored, for there wasn't a single child in the amusement park. Even the open-mouthed wooden horses seemed to be yawning. I found their languor contagious.

"Where are all the children?" I asked.

"They have had enough of swinging," the operator explained. "Come, let's try it," he suggested.

"I guess I am too old for that." I dallied with the idea and shyly mounted a wooden steed with the help of the operator, who then started the motor and quickly sprang upon an elephant next to me.

"I have to fulfill my plan," he admitted.

The merry-go-round began to revolve.

"You must be very bored here," I said.

"How can you think that!" he shouted, offended. "I am carrying out my responsibilities at an accelerated tempo."

"Did you say responsibilities?" I thought that, because of the wind, I had misunderstood his statement.

"Of course. Nowadays we don't have any untrustworthy positions," he confided spurring the elephant. "The speed of every work requires the maximum energy."

The merry-go-round revolved faster and faster, resembling empty grindstones at a mill. My head began to whirl.

"In our system no one can afford to hang back," the operator continued eagerly. "Look, we are progressing. Let's speed forward! Do you agree with me?"

I was unable to open my mouth because of the breakneck velocity.

"Just straight ahead, without any deviation from the course," he shouted into the wind and straddled his elephant like a maharaja. "I have an idea. Let's pledge to achieve six revolutions a minute instead of four!"

I was overpowered by seasickness. My face turned green with fright. Unable to remain in the saddle, I tried to dismount from my horse.

"We don't have any mercy for deserters!" The operator glanced at me and struck my back.

I clung to the neck of my horse in despair.

"That is good," he praised me. "Now you are growing and improving. You are not far from heroism."

The revolutions of the merry-go-round slowly decreased because of the automatic brakes.

"Didn't I operate it courageously?" he asked.

"Sure," I replied, wondering whether I would ever be able to get rid of these whirling sensations. All over the amusement park the operator's voice boomed in triumph, "Four revolutions instead of a half-revolution without any deviation from the course!"

(Aleksis Rubulis)

Bibliography

AISTIS, J., and VAIČIULAITIS, A. *Lietuvių Poezijos Antologija*. Chicago, 1951.

ARISTE, P., ed. *Kalevipoja*. Tartu, 1963.

ARV 20 (1964).

BELIAJUS, VYTAUTAS F., trans. and ed. *The Evening Song: Lithuanian Legends and Fables*. Los Angeles, 1952.

BĒRZIŅŠ, ARTURS. *Jānis Jaunsudrabiņš*. Västerås, 1952.

BEZZENBERGER, A., et al. *Die Osteuropäischen Literaturen und die slawischen Sprachen*. Leipzig, 1908.

BĪLMANIS, ALFREDS. *Latvia As an Independent State*. Washington, 1947.

BLESE, ERNESTS. *Latviešu literātūras vēsture*. Hanau, 1947.

BONSER, WILFRID. "The Mythology of the Kalevala, with Notes on Bearworship Among the Finns." *Folk-Lore* XXXIX (Dec. 1928), 344–358.

BUDDENSIEG, HERMANN. "Kristijonas Donelaitis. Leben und Werk in seiner Zeit." In *Die Jahreszeiten* by Kristijonas Donelaitis. Munich, 1966.

BUKDAHL, JORGEN. "Kalevala." *Scandinavia Past and Present* I (1959), 235–252.

BUKŠS, MIĶELIS. *Vacōki rakstnīceibas pīminekli*. Traunstein, 1952.

ČIURLYS, P. *Litovskije poety XIX veka*. Leningrad, 1962.

COMPARETTI, D. *Der Kalevala*. Halle, 1892.

DRAVNIEKS, A. *Latviešu literātūras vēsture*. Göppingen, 1946.

ĒRMANIS, P., and PLAUDIS, A., eds. *Trimdas rakstnieki*. 3 vols. Kempten, 1947.

FROMM, HANS. *Kalevala: Kommentar*. Munich, 1967.

FULLER, EDMUND. "Akhnaton the Heretic." *The Saturday Review of Literature* XXXII, no. 10 (Aug. 20, 1949), 9–10.

GODENHJELM, B. F. *Handbook of Finnish Literature*. London, 1896.

HARRIS, HOWARD E. *Literature in Estonia*. London, 1947.

HARVEY, ELIZABETH. "The Art of Sillanpää." *The Scandinavian Review* II (1940), 184–195.

HAVU, ILMARI. *An Introduction to Finnish Literature.* Helsinki, 1952.

HEIN, MANFRED P. *Moderne finnische Lyrik.* Göttingen, 1962.

HOWITT, W. "The Heroes of the Kalevala." *The Athenaeum,* 1855, pp. 1434–1435.

IVASK, GEORGE. "Eight Estonian Poets." *Unesco Bulletin of Selected Books,* no. 1, 1968.

JUNGFER, VICTOR. *Litauischer Liederschrein.* Tübingen, 1948.

JÄNES, HENNO. *Geschichte der estnischen Literatur.* Stockholm, 1965.

KALLAS, OSKAR. *Die Wiederholungslieder der estnischen Volkspoesie.* Helsinki, 1901.

KĀRKLIŅŠ, KĀRLIS. *Latviešu literātūras vēsture.* Fischbach, Germany, 1946.

—————. *Rūdolfs Blaumanis.* Waverly, Iowa, 1957.

KIRBY, W. F. *The Hero of Estonia.* 2 vols. London, 1895.

KÕRESSAAR, V., and RANNIT, A., eds. *Estonian Poetry and Language.* Stockholm, 1965.

KORINNA, L. "Alexis Kivi. A Grand Old Man of Finnish Literature." *The Scandinavian Review* I (March, 1939), 328.

KORSAKAS, K., ed. *Lietuvių literatūros istorija.* 3 vols. Vilnius, 1965.

KORSAKAS, K., and LEBEDYS, J., eds. *Lietuvių literatūros istorijos chrestomatija.* Vilnius, 1957.

KOSKULL, JOSI VON., trans. and ed. *Baltische Märchen.* 2 vols. Döhren, 1960.

KREUTZWALD, F. R. *Kalewipoeg.* Translated into German by Carl Reinthal. Dorpat, 1857–1861.

KUBILIUS, V., MARCINKEVIČIUS, J., et al., eds. *Lietuvių poezija.* 2 vols. Vilnius, 1967.

LANDSBERGIS, A., and MILLS, CLARK, eds. *The Green Linden.* New York, 1964.

LIGERS, ZIEDONIS. *Ethnographie lettone.* Basel, 1954.

The Literary Review. VIII, no. 3 (1965).

LÖNNROT, ELIAS. *The Kalevala.* Translated and edited by F. P. Magoun, Jr. Cambridge, Mass., 1963.

—————. *The Kalevala.* Translated and edited by W. F. Kirby. 2 vols. London, 1961.

LÖWIS OF MENAR, AUGUST VON., trans. and ed. *Finnische und estnische Märchen.* Cologne, 1962.

MÄGI, ARVO, ed. *Eesti Lüürika.* 2 vols. Lund, 1958.

—————. *Estonian Literature.* Stockholm, 1968.

MATTHEWS, W. K. *Anthology of Modern Estonian Poetry.* Gainesville, Fla., 1953.

MAUCLÈRE, JEAN. *Littérature lithuanienne.* Paris, 1938.

NIRK, E., ed. *Antologija estonskoi poezii.* 2 vols. Moscow, 1959.

NOREM, OWEN J. C. *Timeless Lithuania.* Cleveland, 1967.

ORAS, ANTS. *Acht estnische Dichter,* Stockholm, 1964.

————. *Estonian Literature in Exile.* Lund, 1967.

————. *Estonian Literary Reader.* Bloomington, 1963.

PRANDE, ALBERTS. *Latvju rakstniecība portrejās.* Riga, 1926.

PROPP, V. J., ed. *Karelskie epicheskie pesni.* Leningrad, 1950.

RANDEL, WILLIAM. "This Man Waltari." *Books Abroad* XXX (1956), 165–167.

RANNNIT, ALEKSIS. "Kristijonas Donelaitis and Lithuanian Poetry. In observance of the 250th anniversary of the birth of Lithuania's classical poet." *Baltic Review* XXX (1965), 48–64.

————. *The Yale Lectures in Estonian Poetry.* New Haven, 1970.

RAUD, VILLIBALD. *Estonia.* New York, 1953.

RUBULIS, ALEKSIS. *Latvian Literature.* Toronto, 1964.

RUMMO, PAUL, ed. *Estonskie poety XIX veka.* Leningrad, 1961.

RUTKIS, J., ed. *Latvia: Country and People.* Stockholm, 1967.

SAARINEN, E. "Movements in Modern Finnish Literature." *The Norseman* XIV (1956), 278–284.

SALU, HERBERT. *Estonian Literature.* Stockholm, 1961.

SARAJAS, ANNAMARI. "Contemporary Finnish Writing." *Books Abroad* XXIX (Spring 1955), 149–154.

Senatne un Māksla II (1937).

SENN, ALFRED E. *The Emergence of Modern Lithuania.* New York, 1959.

TARKKA, PEKKA. "Finnish Literature: the Great Tradition." *Odyssey Review* III (Mar. 1963), 164–172.

TUMAS, ELENA. "Introduction" to *The Seasons* by Kristijonas Donelaitis. Los Angeles, 1967.

TURUNEN, AIMO. *Kalevalan sanakirja.* Helsinki, 1949.

VAIČIULAITIS, ANTANAS. *Outline of Lithuanian Literature.* Chicago, 1942.

VÄISÄNEN, A. O. "The Origin of *Kalevala.*" *The Norseman* VII (1949), 132–134.

VAŠKELIS, BRONIUS. "Vincas Krėvė." *Lituanus* III (1965), 5–14.

WALTERS, M. *Le Peuple Letton.* Riga, 1926.

WILLMANN, ASTA. "The Perceptional World of Aleksis Rannit's Poetry." *Yale Literary Review* XI (1967), 42–60.

ZEIFERTS, TEODORS. *Latviešu rakstniecības vēsture.* 3 vols. Riga, 1922–1925.

ZIEDONIS, ARVIDS, JR. *The Religious Philosophy of Jānis Rainis.* Waverly, Iowa, 1969.

ZOBARSKAS, STEPAS, ed. *Selected Lithuanian Short Stories.* New York, 1963.